Learning from Singap

Learning from Singapore tells the inside story of the country's journey in transforming its education system from a struggling one to one that is hailed internationally as effective and successful. It is a story not of the glory of international test results, but of the hard work and tenacity of a few generations of policy makers, practitioners and teacher trainers. Despite its success, Singapore continues to reform its education system, and is willing to deal with difficult issues and challenges of change. Citing Singapore's transformation, author Pak Tee Ng highlights how context and culture affect education policy formulation and implementation. Showing how difficult education reform can be when a system needs to negotiate between competing philosophies, significant trade-offs, or paradoxical positions, this book explores the successes and struggles of the Singapore system and examines its future direction and areas of tension. The book also explores how national education systems can be strengthened by embracing the creative tensions generated by paradoxes such as the co-existence of timely change and timeless constants, centralisation and decentralisation, meritocracy and compassion, and teaching less and learning more. *Learning from Singapore* brings to the world the learning *from* Singapore—what Singapore has learned from half a century of educational change—and encourages every education system to bring hope to and secure a future for the next generation.

Pak Tee Ng is Associate Dean, Leadership Learning at the National Institute of Education, Nanyang Technological University in Singapore.

The Routledge Leading Change Series
Edited by Andy Hargreaves and Pak Tee Ng

The New Imperatives of Educational Change: Achievement with Integrity
Dennis Shirley

Learning from Singapore: The Power of Paradoxes
Pak Tee Ng

Learning from Singapore
The Power of Paradoxes

Pak Tee Ng

Routledge
Taylor & Francis Group

NEW YORK AND LONDON

First published 2017
by Routledge
711 Third Avenue, New York, NY 10017

and by Routledge
2 Park Square, Milton Park, Abingdon, Oxon, OX14 4RN

Routledge is an imprint of the Taylor & Francis Group, an informa business

© 2017 Taylor & Francis

The right of Pak Tee Ng to be identified as author of this work has been asserted by him in accordance with sections 77 and 78 of the Copyright, Designs and Patents Act 1988.

Library of Congress Cataloging in Publication Data
A catalog record has been requested for this book

ISBN: 978-1-138-92690-5 (hbk)
ISBN: 978-1-138-92691-2 (pbk)
ISBN: 978-1-315-68291-4 (ebk)

Typeset in Adobe Caslon
by Apex CoVantage, LLC

Contents

Acknowledgements

This book is dedicated to educators in Singapore, who persevere on a professional path not easily travelled, to teach other people's children like their own. Singapore has a future because there are educators who tirelessly safeguard that future.

I would like to thank Professor Andy Hargreaves for his excellent leadership of this book series and his helpful advice to me for this book. He is a role model of an accomplished academic who builds others generously.

I would also like to thank Professor Dennis Shirley for his companionship, advice and encouragement along a common journey to become the first two authors to publish a book in the series.

I thank my wife Claudia for loving me selflessly; my parents, sister and brother-in-law for their unwavering support; and my research assistant Maria for helping me with initial drafts of the book. I would also like to thank all who have contributed in one way or another to this book, or in my personal development as an academic and educator.

Above all, I thank God for His grace that sustains me in my life and work.

I

BACKGROUND AND INTRODUCTION

1

INTRODUCTION
The Paradoxical Pictures of Singapore

The Singapore story is one not of the glory of international test results, but of the hard work, tenacity and sacrifice of a few generations of educators.

When 2012 Programme for International Student Assessment (PISA) results were going to be released in December 2013, many education systems went into a frenzy, eagerly waiting for what is now similar to a football World Cup among education systems. When the results were released, there were cheers from some and moans from others. The East Asian systems were hailed by the Organisation for Economic Cooperation and Development (OECD) as shining examples of educational success. Finland was still there at the top but showed signs of slipping in the rankings. The United States and various European countries were given a beating. Some newspapers headlines screamed about the murder of education in the West and others called the PISA results a wake-up call for them.

Singapore was one of the top education systems in the PISA 2012 league table. It was already there in PISA 2009. In fact, Singapore has ranked high since the 1980s in the Trends in International Mathematics and Science Study (TIMSS) and the Progress in International Reading Literacy Study (PIRLS). But it was the 2009 PISA that really pushed the Singapore education system into the limelight, and its credibility is now validated through its repeated excellent performance in the 2012 PISA.[1] In PISA 2012, Singaporean students demonstrated better English reading skills and comprehension compared with English speaking countries such as Canada, New Zealand, Australia, the United States and the UK. Singapore also topped the computer-based assessment of Problem Solving. In 2015, OECD ranked Singapore as the top education system in the world, based on the performance in mathematics and science of students at age 15.[2] Singapore is the new poster child of education systems according to the international league tables.

In addition to shining in these international tests, Singapore students have won many awards at various international competitions and Olympiads. For example, in 2015, Singapore beat 27 countries in the International Young Physicists' Tournament to become the

Table 1.1 Trends in International Mathematics and Science Study (TIMSS)

	LEVEL	MATH	SCIENCE
1995	Grade 3	2nd	7th
	Grade 4	1st	7th
	Grade 7	1st	1st
	Grade 8	1st	1st
1999	Grade 8	1st	2nd
2003	Grade 4	1st	1st
	Grade 8	1st	1st
2007	Grade 4	2nd	1st
	Grade 8	3rd	1st
2011	Grade 4	1st	2nd
	Grade 8	2nd	1st

Table 1.2 Progress in International Reading Literacy Study (PIRLS)

	RANKING
2001	15th
2006	4th
2011	4th

Table 1.3 PISA 2009

SUBJECTS	RANKING
Math	2nd
Science	4th
Reading	5th

Table 1.4 PISA 2012

	RANKING
Math	2nd
Science	3rd
Reading	3rd
Computer-based assessment on problem solving	1st

first country to be champions for three consecutive years. Singapore also won three gold medals and one silver medal, placing third out of 60 countries that competed in the 26th International Biology Olympiad.[3] At the 27th World Schools Debating Championship, the Singapore team beat 53 other nations and 250 participants to become champion.[4] In 2014, at the 10th ASEAN Skills Competition held in Vietnam, the Singapore student delegation won a total of 11 medals, in categories such as Mobile Robotics, Beauty Therapy, Information Network Cabling and Restaurant Service.[5] In the November 2015 International Baccalaureate (IB) diploma examinations, Singapore produced more than half of the students with perfect scores.[6]

The success story of Singapore has generated interest around the world. Over the years, interested parties from overseas have asked me many pertinent questions. Some examples are listed in Table 1.5.

As a lifelong citizen and resident of Singapore, I am proud of my country and its education system, of which I am a part. If you are not Singaporean but feel that Singapore has a great education system, I thank you. But as a citizen and an educator in Singapore, I think the fact that we are ranked highly in international league tables means quite simply that we are ranked highly in international league tables. It does not mean that we have arrived at where we would like to be. It is of course better to be at the top of these rankings than to be at the bottom. But international rankings are not what we are aiming for. We are more interested in the actual education of our children and young people. Even when we are ranked highly in the league tables, we know that we still need to do a lot more to get better. There are many areas for improvement, and we have plenty of work ahead of us. Our educators face challenges on a daily basis. Our education system is always a work in progress.

Table 1.5 Examples of questions I have received

QUESTION	MY QUICK RESPONSE
What did Singapore do to gain such success in the international league tables?	I have my way of explaining this but the more interesting question is, What does Singapore do now that it is at the top of these league tables? Read Chapter 3 for more details.
In competitive Singapore, don't children from disadvantaged backgrounds fall through the cracks in the education system?	There is every danger of that, and that is what Singapore has been trying very hard to prevent, especially in recent years. Read Chapter 4 for more details.
Singapore has a top-down education system. Do school leaders and teachers get to exercise professional autonomy?	Yes, school leaders and teachers exercise autonomy, but always in a manner aligned to national needs and goals. Read Chapter 5 for more details.
Does educational reform in Singapore reach into classrooms to affect teaching and learning?	We are trying very hard to do this, but it is not easy. We are very cognisant that reform is not just about changing structures. Read Chapter 6 for more details.

I have given numerous keynote speeches at conferences around the world and have told the Singapore story many times. I have explained our policy changes, the way we develop our school leaders and teachers, and how we revamp our curriculum and pedagogy. Had Singapore not been deemed as successful in the eyes of the world, I would not have received those invitations. I was a beneficiary of my country's education system and now a beneficiary of its success. I was educated up to the post-secondary level in our school system. Then I was awarded a scholarship to go to Cambridge University for mathematics as an undergraduate. I returned to Singapore to serve as a mathematics teacher in a junior college (for students age 17–18). Without a scholarship sponsored by my country, my family would have found it quite difficult to afford an overseas education for me. I taught for a few years, before being transferred to the Ministry of Education (MOE) to become an MOE officer. After a few years at the MOE, I joined the National Institute of Education (NIE) as an academic. The NIE, which is part of Nanyang Technological University (NTU), is the only education university-institute in the country and has a national remit to train all teachers and leaders for the school system. The MOE, NIE and schools work very closely in a tri-partite partnership that ensures congruence of policy, preparation and practice. My main area of teaching and research is now educational policy and leadership, and one of my main roles is the training and development of school and teacher leaders for my country.

This book tells the story of the Singapore education system. It is a story not of the glory of international test results, but of the hard work and tenacity of a few generations of policy makers, practitioners and teacher trainers. It is a story of how educators bit the bullet to implement far-sighted policies, and how Singapore has made hard decisions to transform an education system from a poor one in the 1960s to what it is today. Singapore, as we shall see, is still dealing with difficult issues and imperfections, even when it seems to have developed a successful education system. Its story is situated within a bigger narrative of a country that survived against the odds for half a century, and that has every intention to do so for many centuries more.

This book highlights how context and culture affect education policy formulation and implementation. Singapore's success and challenges show how difficult education reform can be when a system needs to negotiate among competing philosophies, significant trade-offs and paradoxical positions. Singapore does not treat seemingly conflicting educational philosophies as dichotomies, thereby adopting an extreme position, nor does it debate endlessly the virtues (or otherwise) of these philosophies. Rather, Singapore embraces and draws strength from the creative tensions generated by these paradoxes. The paradoxes include the co-existence of timely change and timeless constants, centralisation and decentralisation, meritocracy and compassion, and teaching less to learn more. I will expound on these paradoxes in the later chapters.

This book is not a chronicle or a comprehensive review of the Singapore education system. Nor does it champion the 'Singapore model' as a model for other education systems. The so-called Singapore model is rather Singaporean and emerges because of its history and context. Even so, there is a great deal that the world can learn from Singapore's experience. What Singapore has done (like what Finland has done) can trigger ideas for real and substantial points of departure for school improvement in other countries. The book draws out lessons for others as it explores the successes and struggles of the Singapore system (especially in recent years) and examines its future direction and areas of tension. This book hopes to stimulate reflection and generate discussion among teachers, school leaders, academics, researchers and educational policy makers, both locally and internationally, regarding educational change, using Singapore as a case study.

The Approach of This Book

Many policy makers, educational leaders, academics and researchers will have read some of the many international reports regarding the Singapore education system. These are good reports which offer insights from various perspectives. This book does something different.

I write as a citizen of the country, a teacher-educator in the education system and an academic in a local university. I am born and bred in Singapore. Both my parents are retired teachers here. You can imagine the teacher stories I have heard since I was young! Add those to the teacher stories that I have accumulated over the past two decades working closely with school leaders and teachers in the education system, and I believe I have the advantage of an inside perspective. In my role at the NIE, I get to interact with teachers and school leaders from every school in Singapore. Because Singapore is such a small country, I have taught half its current school principals through the leadership programmes at the NIE. Before I retire, I might have taught all the principals serving at that point in time! I am privileged and grateful to be given the opportunity to do so.

These practitioners tell me about the wonderful things that they do in school. They also tell me the many challenges that they face. I get a front row seat to observe change in the education system and in schools over many years. This helps me gain a clearer and richer picture of the education system in Singapore. At the same time, in my academic work, I have the privilege to interact with my many friends overseas, which also helps me appreciate and adopt an outsider view of the system. I deeply appreciate these friends and colleagues for helping me sharpen this insider-outsider perspective of Singapore and its education system.

Analyses contained in many international reports of educational policy tend to adopt a macro perspective. Their conclusions are often generalised as key success strategies for others to learn from. The lessons to be learned from Singapore, according to these reports, include the following:

- *Long term view*: Singapore is prepared to develop and implement education policies that will only bear fruit in 5, 10 or even 20 to 30 years.
- *Fidelity*: The Singapore ministry works closely with schools to communicate policy intentions. Schools implement policies with support from the ministry and are in alignment with its overall direction.
- *Social and economic development*: Singapore invests heavily in education and aligns its education system to support social and economic development.
- *Boldness*: Singapore makes bold system level interventions when necessary to drive and support further change.
- *Meritocracy*: Singapore students have opportunities for success and advancement regardless of race and religion.
- *Equity*: Singapore is committed to reducing achievement gaps, by putting in programmes and support structures to level up those who are struggling or falling behind.
- *High standards*: Singapore maintains rigorous academic standards and high stakes examinations.
- *Professional capital*: Singapore employs high quality teachers and principals. It recruits from the top one-third of each graduating cohort and invests heavily in professional development. It develops systematic career paths for educators and grooms promising ones for leadership positions.
- *High status of education*: Singapore has a culture where education is valued by parents and the society. This provides great support for educational advancement and attainment.
- *Accountability*: Singapore is committed to strong school accountability. There is a well-developed school self-evaluation system, coupled with a national system of school awards. Schools are conversant with annual cycles of target setting, implementation, data collection, evaluation and improvement.
- *Global learning*: Singapore is adept at learning from other systems overseas and adapting ideas. It sends its officers overseas on learning visits and adapts relevant practices appropriately.

These are all very good and helpful points. They seem like they could be transposed to other systems easily. But, as we shall see, the details reveal very different constraints and possibilities. For example, it is often mentioned that Singapore employs high quality teachers. Many people ask me how Singapore schools can attract such good quality candidates. But, actually, schools do not do that. In Singapore, it is the MOE that employs teachers for the whole country. Teachers are hired by the MOE even before they are sent to the NIE for teacher training. Throughout their training at the NIE, trainee teachers are already paid a salary and their education fees are fully borne by the MOE. They sign a three-year bond with the MOE to work as a teacher in a local school. The MOE posts the teachers who have been trained to the various schools based on the needs of the school. Therefore, the system in Singapore is quite different from those in many parts of the world, where teachers pay for their own training and then try to look for a job at a school after graduation. In Singapore, teachers are *posted* to schools after training, and they are *guaranteed* a job! Teachers in Singapore sign up for a profession, not a school. They do not know when they sign up which school they will be teaching at (except that they will become primary or secondary school teachers). Therefore, Singapore teachers are expected to be adaptable and to work with students from different backgrounds, regardless of their own. They can be posted to a school where students come from homes that are very different from their own.

Moreover, generalised lessons of success may 'hide' certain human dynamics and subtle tensions within a system like Singapore's. For example, the 2012 PISA results indicated that Singapore students read better in English compared with some countries which are native users of the language. If you visit Singapore as a tourist, you will find that you are able to use English to communicate with Singaporeans everywhere you go. So the use of English in teaching is usually portrayed as a source of strength in the Singapore education system. But many teachers in the 1960s could not use English to teach. There was a lot of hard work and there were painful trade-offs to get to this stage where English is Singapore's lingua franca. Even now, the country is doing a lot to support students who are not from English speaking backgrounds. A generalised statement does not adequately reflect the internal dynamics, challenges and trajectories of change.

The supposed key success factors of the Singapore education system are not always, in reality, obviously or one-dimensionally positive or negative. There is a richer reality to these key success factors. In fact, certain aspects can be puzzling or paradoxical. For example, Singapore schools would like to develop more creativity in their students, but they also want their students to do well in standardised tests. Singapore encourages and supports schools to differentiate themselves from and even compete with one another based on their areas of strength, but Singapore runs a highly centralised system at the same time. These are not contradictions to be resolved. They are paradoxes to be appreciated. Indeed, these paradoxes are the creative tensions that drive great change.

Paradoxes and Perspectives

This book tells the Singapore story through some of the paradoxes found in its education system. Paradoxes are 'normal'. They help us appreciate certain ideas or realities better. For example, scientists accept and appreciate that the wave-particle duality of light is paradoxical. So, many paradoxes are actually 'sensible'.

Consider the following contrasting pictures of the Singapore education system. On one hand, Singapore implements policies with careful planning, resource support and great levels of fidelity. On the other hand, some teachers in school complain that implementation is a rough ride. The question is, which is the real picture? Well, both are real! As a system, Singapore is excellent at planning, resourcing and implementing policies. But this does not mean a smooth ride for every teacher. Let us consider a smoothly flowing river. At the macro level, a person sitting beside the river remarks, "What peaceful waters!" But if you are a water molecule in the middle of the river, you will not see things that way! You will be bombarded by other water molecules and screaming "Chaos!" That is the difference arising from the different levels of perspective. Now, if you would like the river to change course, you would put in a structure such as a dam. The river changes course. Your macro level intervention works. The river now flows in a certain direction, as you would like it. People will interview you for your key success factors. But if you could observe the movement of each water molecule, you may find it hard to discern a pattern. In the same way, observed from a macro point of view, a policy has just changed the course of a system and worked like a charm. Observed from a micro point of view, the situation is a lot messier. So, which is the real picture? Herein lies the paradox. Both pictures, seemingly contradictory, are real and valid. A policy intervention may have an effect on the direction of system movement. This does not guarantee that the direction of movement of every individual is the same as that of the system. Indeed, some people's experience may be the exact opposite of what the policy intervention is supposed to achieve. There are many layers of reality to the intricacies of educational change.

How about statistics? Figures do not lie, right? Well, that is partly true. According to the PISA results, Singapore students are doing pretty well. But for some students, this is at odds with what they experience as their difficulties in learning or their lack of desirable examination results. Is there something wrong with trusting figures? Take two classes, A and B, each with two students. In class A, each student scores 50. In class B, one student scores 100 and the other scores 0. Both classes have a mean score of 50. Obviously, they are very different classes. Most of the time, headlines and leagues tables reflect only the mean scores, which tell a story, but not necessarily the complete one. Singapore has such high mean scores in PISA that many observers have not noticed the country's 'long tail' of students who are performing well below average. But, as we will see in Chapter 4, the system is now doing something about it. If observers visit only Singapore's top schools, they will miss some of the best things that have happened in the education system. What the top schools do for students who are excelling in their studies is great. But what the average schools do for students who are struggling is more illustrative of Singapore's recent focus.

Let's look more closely at some of the metrics that are used to compare Singapore with other education systems, such as Finland. The media in Singapore has carried reports about Finland's successful education system. There are no national exams until the age of 18 in Finland. Private tuition is unheard of. Now, is that not an education utopia? The media has also carried reports about Singapore's own education system. There are high stakes standardised examinations starting from the age of 12. Private tuition is ubiquitous. Is that not an education pressure cooker? Yet, in a recent OECD report, a significantly higher percentage of Singapore students reported that they were happy in school (87.9%) compared to their Finnish counterparts (66.9%) (the OECD average was 79.8%).[7]

But let's not jump to simplistic conclusions. I spoke with a primary school boy recently and asked him whether he liked his school. He answered "yes" emphatically. He told me he liked his friends and some of his teachers. I asked him whether he felt stressed in school. He said, "Not during PE [physical education] lessons or recess time!" Then he told me he was stressed during tests and examinations because he had to study, but otherwise, "School is OK!" Was he happy? Yes. Was he stressed? Yes. I wonder how this child would respond to a survey question of whether he was happy in school.

None of this says that figures are not useful. Figures are necessary pointers to tell us how an education system is doing overall. However, such figures, when taken as generalisations, may lead people to miss out on other aspects of the system. It takes great empathy to understand that even when failure figures are low, the failure rate feels like 100% to a particular student who has failed. This is the sort of empathy that is necessary to help those individuals who are left behind, even in a successful education system.

How should we interpret another set of statistics that point to Singaporean students' skills at problem solving? According to the 2012 PISA results, Singaporean students are the best problem solvers in the world.[8] But are they not 'reputed' to be rote learners who memorise facts and over-practice examination questions? Singapore's education system is undergoing change from an old paradigm to a new one, where two contrasting states exist at the same time. There are examples of activities that illustrate the essence of the new paradigm. But the old paradigm is still dominant. So, Singapore has both students who are problem solvers and students who are rote learners. It even has students who are both problem solvers *and* rote learners. One has to embrace multiple layers of realities, manifested in seemingly contradictory pictures and accounts, in order to appreciate more completely the subtleties of change. But paradoxes like these are two sides of the same coin, not two ends of a continuum. They provide the creative tensions to drive change. The dissonance they create can generate new ideas. Finding the 'secrets' of Singapore's success is impossible without adopting different perspectives, grasping different levels of reality, and embracing its paradoxes. Indeed, these very paradoxes help Singapore evolve into a better system.

One last point about perspective: the nature of my own! This book shares my reflections on the Singapore education system. I will describe the dynamics of change through some examples on the ground. I will also use a lot of quotes from the key speeches of political leaders. In Singapore, these key speeches are actually the 'official' communiqué of the government. They express the content of policy documents in lay terms, making it easy for the public to understand. Official policy documents, with a lot of implementation details, are often kept confidential among the officials. I have conducted research with many teachers and school leaders about their perspectives on education policy and practice. I draw upon the findings of these research projects to inform the content of this book and share quotes from teachers and school leaders who participated in the research. I am also attentive to the perspectives of many officials, other researchers and international academics. But, in the end, this book rests on my own perspective. It is by no means an authoritative account. While I try to be evidence-based, analytical and objective, I am deeply mindful that this book is shaped by my own identity, values and worldview.

Structure of the Book

This book comprises a total of 11 chapters that are divided into 4 sections. Section I, 'Background and Introduction', comprises Chapters 1 and 2. Section II, 'The Four Paradoxes', comprises Chapters 3 to 6. Section III, 'The Four Dreams', comprises Chapters 7 to 10. Section IV, 'Conclusion', comprises Chapter 11. This beginning chapter has provided an introduction to the book and some of its key ideas, including an overview of the key success factors of the Singapore education system. However, I hope you will appreciate the idea of paradoxes and the multiple layers of realities in the Singapore success story, and the dangers of using the Singapore system as a model for the rest of the world without understanding its context.

Chapter 2 provides a brief introduction to the physical, social, economic, political and historical aspects of Singapore. It also provides an overview of Singapore's education system and its different phases of development, which helps explain how the Singapore education system reaches its present point of development.

The next section of the book comprises four chapters, each presenting a specific paradox, as follows:

- Timely Change, Timeless Constants
- Compassionate Meritocracy
- Centralised Decentralisation
- Teach Less, Learn More

Why these four paradoxes? In a way, there are many paradoxes and they can be presented in many ways. However, I have decided to explore one paradox in each of the following aspect of education: philosophy of change, educational equity, management of school system, and teaching and learning.

Chapter 3 presents the first paradox 'Timely Change, Timeless Constants', which concerns Singapore's philosophy of change. Singapore is a land where 'some things just keep changing' and 'some things just don't change'. It has to change the formula that has gained it success. What has been a strategy for current success is now a ticket to future failure. Instead of examination results, Singapore is aiming for quality education that can equip young people with knowledge, skills and values for the future. But Singapore is also clinging to certain timeless constants, values that serve as its anchor so that its people will not be lost in the waves of change. It takes courage to change while one is successful, and it takes wisdom to know what not to change as well.

Chapter 4 presents the second paradox, 'Compassionate Meritocracy', which concerns the particular way that Singapore adopts to address the issue of educational equity. Singapore is very strict on its meritocratic principle. People should find success based on merit, and not on ascriptive considerations of race, language or religion. However, in the education system, there are students who may be left behind in this fiercely competitive meritocracy. This chapter explains what Singapore does to help them, so that they have a chance to find success too. There is a compassionate side to Singapore's meritocratic system, and there is an effort to develop this compassionate side further.

Chapter 5 presents the third paradox, 'Centralised Decentralisation', which concerns how the education system is managed. Singapore is both a centralised system, as well as a decentralised one. It centralises to achieve system level synergies. It decentralises so that each school may cater to the students that it serves. I call this approach 'centralised decentralisation'. This chapter explains how Singapore school leaders are adept at balancing the needs of both the system and the school. It also explains how schools are both competitive and collaborative, and how educators are both highly accountable and highly responsible, all at the same time.

Chapter 6 presents the fourth paradox, 'Teach Less, Learn More', which concerns teaching and learning. Singapore aims to teach less so that students can learn more. This chapter explains how Singapore teachers have been teaching too much and how there is now an effort to move away from a focus on quantity to a focus on quality. The aim is to encourage teachers to reflect on their teaching and for students to become engaged learners. Singapore does not engage in education reform by merely making structural changes. It actively tries to influence the teaching and learning dynamics in the classroom.

The next section of the book comprises four more chapters, with each presenting a vision or a 'dream' of the Singapore education system. These four visions, originally presented during the 2012 MOE Work Plan Seminar by Heng Swee Keat[9] (who was at that time the Education Minister) are as follows:

- Every School, a Good School
- Every Student, an Engaged Learner
- Every Teacher, a Caring Educator
- Every Parent, a Supportive Partner

Each of the four statements represents a dream of the Singapore education system. The sum of these four dreams in turn composes a vision that the education system is working towards, articulated not in terms of measurable targets but in relation to shifts in mindsets or reminders of the enduring spirit of education. I found this an excellent framework to discuss the future direction of the Singapore education system.

Chapter 7 presents Singapore's first dream, 'Every School, a Good School'. While there are no failing schools in Singapore, parents are competing to get their children into elite schools. So, how does a country get its citizens to buy into the idea that any school that their child may go to is a good one? This chapter examines the issues and challenges associated with 'every school, a good school', and what the country is doing to realise this vision.

Chapter 8 presents Singapore's second dream, 'Every Student, an Engaged Learner'. Singapore students are generally hard-working and can do well in examinations. But they are also rather stressed and may not be engaged in the learning process. This chapter examines how the education system is attempting to change what is probably the most difficult aspect of education reform—creating the environment for engaged learning against a backdrop of high stakes examinations and academic pressure.

Chapter 9 presents Singapore's third dream, 'Every Teacher, a Caring Educator'. Singapore has a reputation of having a high quality teaching force. Teachers work very hard, and they care about their students. However, their load is heavy and they feel stressed. In Singapore, caring is not just an act of individual will but the effort of an entire community of educators. This chapter examines what the system is trying to do to support every teacher to be a caring educator in a sustainable way.

Chapter 10 presents Singapore's fourth dream, 'Every Parent, a Supportive Partner'. Singapore parents value education. But as Singapore modernises, parents have rising expectations of schools, and different parents have different opinions about how education should be conducted. Some schools find that it is increasingly difficult to deal with parents and satisfy their expectations. Parents are anxious about their children's examination results, and such anxiety is not helpful to promoting holistic education. This chapter examines what Singapore is doing to engage parents more fully and change their mindsets regarding educational success.

The book ends with a concluding chapter about the lessons that one can distil from Singapore's experience with educational change. The chapter argues that these lessons are not just about the policies and practices in Singapore, but about how Singapore's paradoxes are powerful in driving change. The chapter points to the commitment and tenacity of Singapore to see through meaningful and long term education reform. But every country or jurisdiction is different, and each will have to find its own path. The state of education reflects what society values, and positive educational change is the result of soul searching on the part of the society.

> International rankings are not what we are aiming for.
>
> **We** are more interested in the actual education of our children and young people.

References

1 Organization for Economic Cooperation and Development (OECD) (2013). *PISA 2012 Results in Focus: What 15-Year-Olds Know and What They Can Do with What They Know.* Paris: PISA, OECD Publishing.
2 Ng, J. Y. (2015, May 14). Singapore tops OECD's global education ranking: Report. Retrieved from http://www.channelnewsasia.com/news/singapore/ singapore-tops-oecd-s/1843546.html
3 Ministry of Education (MOE) (2015, August 11). Outstanding Performance by Singapore at the 2015 International Science and Mathematics Competitions. Press Release. Retrieved from http://www.moe.gov.sg/ media/press/2015/08/outstanding-performance-by-singapore-at-the-2015- international-science-and-mathematics-competitions.php
4 Ministry of Education (MOE) (2015, August 6). Singapore Team Wins 27th World Schools Debating Championship. Press Release. Retrieved from http://www.moe.gov.sg/media/press/2015/08/singapore-team-wins-27th- world-debating-championship.php
5 WorldSkills Singapore (2014, October 28). Singapore Garners Six Gold Medals at the 10th ASEAN Skills Competition in Hanoi, Vietnam. Press Release. Retrieved from https://www.worldskills.sg/wp-content/ uploads/2014/10/ASC-2014-News-Release-final.pdf
6 Teng, A. (2016, January 5). Over half of IB top scorers from S'pore. *The Straits Times*, p. B4.
7 Organization for Economic Cooperation and Development (OECD) (2013). *PISA 2012 Results: Ready to Learn: Students Engagement, Drive and Self-Beliefs* (Volume 3). Paris: PISA, OECD Publishing.
8 Organization for Economic Cooperation and Development (OECD) (2014). *Results from PISA 2012 Problem Solving: Country Note: Singapore.* Paris: PISA, OECD Publishing.
9 Heng, S. K. (2012, September 12). Keynote Address by Mr Heng Swee Keat, Minister for Education, at the Ministry of Education Work Plan Seminar, at Ngee Ann Polytechnic Convention Centre, Singapore.

2

SINGAPORE AND ITS EDUCATION SYSTEM

The first impression of Singapore for most international visitors is the Changi International Airport. A paragon of modern and traveller-friendly features, this airport, which has won more than 400 awards since the 1980s, tells you something about the country.

Changi Airport is beautifully landscaped. The shops, restaurants and restrooms are well designed and strategically placed. There is a two-level butterfly garden with butterflies and orchids. There are even games to help weary parents entertain their children. Wireless internet access is freely available throughout the airport. It is a place where Singaporeans can bring their families for a day outing (not to take a flight!). But it is not just about visual appeal or customer convenience. It actually works. It works smoothly, like a well-oiled clock. From passengers checking in to planes taking off, the airport exudes confidence and efficiency. If a visitor stands around the airport looking lost, one of more than 200 iPad carrying Changi Experience Agents will offer assistance with a smile. In a way, Changi Airport is a reflection of Singapore's mentality. It shows Singapore's spirit to the rest of the world. It blends technocracy with humanity. It is man-made. But it is also charming.

Singapore—The Island Nation

It was not always like this. In 1819, Sir Stamford Raffles established a British port on the island and Singapore became a British colony focusing on entrepôt trade. Singapore was conquered by the Japanese from 1942 to 1945 during the Second World War, but reverted to British rule when the war ended. In 1959, although still a British colony, it gained self-governing status. In 1963, Singapore merged with the Federation of Malaya to form Malaysia. On 9 August 1965, because of political disagreements between the two governments at that time, Singapore separated from Malaysia to become a sovereign nation. The 1960s were difficult times. There were social unrests, severe unemployment and a housing shortage. Educational levels were low. Singapore embarked on a nation building journey that focused initially on rapid industrialisation, housing development, military defence and investment in basic education. Singapore's industrialisation programme began with factories producing basic goods such as garments, textiles, toys and wood products. The government wooed foreign investors willing to develop its export-oriented industries. Positive results began to show as early as the 1970s. Over the next few decades, Singapore's economy surged ahead. Factories were built and skilled manpower was developed. Industries began to diversify and upgrade in technology and value. Singapore's economic structure became more complex with a wide range of businesses, comprising both multi-nationals and local small and medium enterprises. Due to rising land cost and wages, Singapore has to keep moving up the value chain to concentrate on high technology industries and high level services. New areas of growth include industries such as the pharmaceutical biotechnology and medical technology, and services such as banking and healthcare.

The role of the state is prominent in Singapore's rapid economic progress. State-planned economic policies were effectively implemented by the nation's economic institutions. Singapore's economy was built on a few basic tenets: fiscal discipline, good governance, rule of law, and a widely accepted social contract. Singapore's economic transformation over five decades was hailed globally as spectacular, considering its small size, lack of natural resources, and the difficult conditions during the country's early days.

When Deng Xiaoping visited Singapore in November 1978 (his first and only visit), the accomplishments of Singapore which he saw during the visit changed the course of economic development policy in China. Singapore became the model for special economic zones in

China that were opened to foreign trade and investment, paving the way for China to join the World Trade Organization (WTO) in 2001. There was a story that during that visit, then Prime Minister Lee Kuan Yew, despite his personal dislike for cigarette smoke, provided a new spittoon in a well-ventilated meeting room so that Deng, a heavy smoker who used the spittoon, could smoke and spit. But Deng did not smoke or use the spittoon. They both showed great respect for each other.[1] In fact, during a visit to Guangdong Province in 1992, Deng Xiaoping told the Chinese to learn from the world, especially from Singapore. Singapore was hailed as a country with good social order and disciplined governance. Many high level Chinese officials now come to Singapore each year to attend the 'Mayors' Class' at the Nanyang Technological University. In 2015, Singapore played the role of an honest broker to help bring different parties to mutual agreement for the global climate change summit in Paris. Such is the role that Singapore plays on the world stage, even though it is such a small country.

Singapore has grown tremendously since its independence in 1965. The once-grey waterfront for entrepôt trade is now replaced by modern success symbols, such as the Marina Bay Sands complex with its celebrity chef restaurants and an infinity pool on the 57th floor, complete with palm trees overlooking the skyline. The once embattled island is now a venue for the illustrious Formula One World Championship. The first Formula One night race in the world has emerged as one of the most glamorous Formula One events, broadcasting the impressive Singapore night skyline to millions globally. Already reputed to be a garden city, the island is poised to remake itself. The 2013 masterplan for urban renewal envisages towns that are green, healthy and connected, and includes action plans for an environmentally friendly city centre, continuous waterfront promenades, parks within 400 metres of most homes, intra-town networks of cycling tracks and conservation of heritage sites. There are also plans for a new airport terminal and a new port site for ocean-going ships.

Physically, this country is actually a small island. Located south of the Malaya Peninsula in Southeast Asia, it has a population of about 5.3 million and a land area of only about 700 square kilometres. There are ongoing land reclamation projects, which have increased

Singapore's land area from approximately 580 square kilometres in the 1960s to what it is today. It may grow to 800 square kilometres by 2030.

If one resides in a big country, it is hard to imagine how small this country is. During conferences, I usually tell an international audience that if you fly into Singapore and the pilot of your plane misses the Changi International Airport by over-flying for just five minutes, your plane may now very well be flying over another country. Singapore does not have domestic flights. In a big country, such as the United States, Canada, China or Australia, where would you be if you drove on a straight highway at 100 km/h for an hour? Probably nowhere! In Singapore, if you could actually maintain a speed of 100 km/h in a straight line (which would be over Singapore's speed limit of 90km/h and impossible in rush hour congestion), you will drop into the sea in half an hour, no matter where you start on the island. That is how small Singapore is.

Government statistics show that the population in Singapore in 2014 comprises 74.3% Chinese, 13.3% Malay, 9.1% Indian and 3.3% others, each with their own indigenous languages.[2] There are also many religions in the country. The main ones are Buddhism, Islam, Christianity, Catholicism, Taoism and Hinduism.

Singapore is a parliamentary representative democratic republic, modelled generally after the British system. General elections take place once every five years. Since independence in 1965, the People's Action Party (PAP) has been the ruling party in the country. Lee Kuan Yew was the first prime minister of Singapore. Goh Chok Tong took over from Lee Kuan Yew in 1990 and Lee Hsien Loong took over from Goh Chok Tong in 2004. In the 2011 general election, the PAP garnered 60.14% of the votes. In the 2015 general election, the PAP garnered 69.86% of the votes.

Since its independence in 1965, Singapore has achieved one of the most impressive economic growth records globally, averaging 8% gross domestic product (GDP) growth annually from 1960 to 2010. Singapore's GDP per capital was below US$500 in the early years of the 1960s. This grew to US$900 in 1970, US$5,000 in 1980, US$13,000 in 1990, US$24,000 in 2000 and US$47,000 in 2010. That is an incredible rate of growth. The figure was US$56,000 in 2014, and Singapore is one of the top countries in the world in terms of GDP per capita. The literacy rate for residents 15 years old and above is 96.7%.[3]

Because it does not have any natural resources, human resources become Singapore's competitive advantage in the global marketplace, as it jostles with the rest of the world in high technology and high value-adding service industries.

The Singapore Education System

With approximately 370 schools and half a million students, Singapore's education system is basically a public education system. Students receive six years of primary education and four to five years of secondary education. Beyond that, students have a choice of furthering their education in junior colleges, institutes of technical education, polytechnics and ultimately universities. A reader can always find out more details from the Singapore Ministry of Education website.[4] Recent changes reveal a gradual shift from a one-size-fits-all system to a more diversified one. This move is to allow more flexibility to cater to different learners and help them find success in their own ways.

Administratively, there is only one Ministry of Education (MOE) that oversees all public schools in Singapore. The country is divided into four zones (North, South, East and West), each headed by a Zonal Director. Each zone is subdivided into approximately seven school clusters, each headed by a Cluster Superintendent. Each cluster is made up of approximately 12 to 13 schools, usually a mix of primary schools, secondary schools and junior colleges. The Cluster Superintendents develop, guide and supervise the principal and school leadership team in each school in their cluster. The school cluster system encourages networking, sharing and collaboration among the member schools within the cluster to raise the quality of schooling.

The Singapore education community is tightly knit. It is high on social capital.[5] There is a regular and deliberate movement of professionals from one part of the education system to another (amongst MOE, NIE and schools). This dynamic movement helps establish better communication, coordination and understanding among policy makers, academics and practitioners in the education system, a feature that is not often found in other countries.[6]

The government invests significantly in education. The fiscal spending on education is second only to defence. However, as a percentage of GDP, the Singapore figure is strangely lower than the OECD average. Former Education Minister Heng Swee Kiat explained:[7]

> Expenditure on education has increased over the past 5 years by 40%—from $7.5 billion in Financial Year 2007 to $10.5 billion in Financial Year 2012, equivalent to 3.1% of our GDP, and accounting for more than 20% of government expenditure. While OECD countries and other top performing education systems (as measured by PISA) spend between 4–7% of GDP on education, but because their governments tax and spend more as a percentage of GDP, expenditure on education makes up, on average, only about 13% of their government expenditure—significantly less than Singapore.

In a way, given the good outcomes for Singapore students, this suggests that Singapore does not pump resources extravagantly into the education system, but rather makes effective use of the resources across the system. While educational funding has been generous, school leaders are required to be prudent and judicious in financial matters. Singapore generally derives a good value for its money from its schools.

The education system in Singapore aims to help children develop a passion for lifelong learning, build self-confidence, discover their own talents and realise their potential. The Compulsory Education Act ensures that every Singaporean child above the age of 6 and below the age of 15 receives primary education. Public education is highly affordable in Singapore.

Primary education in Singapore, normally starting at age seven, is made up of a four-year foundation stage from Primary 1 to 4 and a two-year orientation stage from Primary 5 to 6. In order to provide students with a holistic learning experience, the primary school curriculum covers three main aspects of education: subject disciplines, knowledge skills and character development. Subject disciplines comprise subject areas such as languages (English and mother tongue), mathematics, science (which is taught from Primary 3 onwards), humanities and the arts. Knowledge skills develop students' thinking processes and communication, through studying a variety of subjects and working on different projects. Character development is facilitated through teacher-pupil interactions, character and citizenship education (CCE), co-curricular activities (CCA) and physical education (PE).

As different children have different aptitudes, capabilities and talents, subject-based banding, which starts in Primary 5 and continues until Primary 6, was introduced in 2008 to offer greater individual flexibility by giving students the choice to take a combination of standard or foundation subjects, depending on their strengths. For example, if their strengths are English and mother tongue but not mathematics and science, they may choose to take the first two subjects at the standard level and the others at the foundation level. This will enable them to progress faster in the subjects that they are strong in and have a slower learning pace to build up the fundamentals in the subjects they are weak in.

More concretely, at the end of Primary 4, based on the children's school-based examination results, their school recommends a subject combination for them. Their parents fill in an option form, indicating the preferred subject combination for their Primary 5 education. At the end of Primary 5, if they are able to do very well in one or more foundation subject(s), they may be permitted by their school to upgrade one or two of those subjects to standard level in Primary 6. On the other hand, if children who take four standard subjects but could not cope well with some of them, they may be advised to take those subjects at foundation level in Primary 6.[8]

After completing six years of primary education, students sit for a national level standardised examination called the Primary School Leaving Examination (PSLE). The PSLE is at the centre of many public debates in the media because it is seen as giving children stress and making parents anxious (read Chapters 8 and 10). Upon the release of the PSLE results, students and their parents are encouraged by the MOE to choose a secondary school that matches the students' learning needs and one that is near their homes. Each student makes six school choices in rank order of preference. Allocation to a school is based on each student's merit and choice. Generally speaking, the better the student's results, the higher the chance of getting into the secondary school that the student has chosen.

There is an exception to this process. The Direct School Admission—Secondary (DSA-Sec) Exercise was introduced in 2004 to encourage students with special talents to spend more time and effort in developing their talents. Participating secondary schools are now allowed to use school-based criteria to choose a certain number of students based on their achievements and special talents for admission to Secondary 1, before these students take the PSLE. Students admitted under the DSA-Sec Exercise are not allowed to transfer to another school after the release of their PSLE results because they need to honour their commitment to their allocated DSA-Sec schools. The majority of Primary 6 students, however, participate in the Secondary One Posting Exercise after the release of the PSLE results. An overview of Singapore's primary education is presented in Figure 2.1.

After completing six years of primary education, students begin their secondary school journey. Based on their PSLE results, students are placed in the Express Course, Normal (Academic) Course or Normal (Technical) Course. While students may begin their secondary education in a particular course, they are given chances, based on their results, to make a lateral transfer mid-stream to a more suitable course that matches their rate of progress. For example, a student who performs well at the end of Secondary 1 Normal (Academic) will have the flexibility to transfer to Secondary 2 Express. An overview of the Singapore's secondary education and post-secondary education is presented in Figure 2.2.

Students in the Express Course study a four-year curriculum that leads to the General Certificate of Education (GCE) Ordinary Level ('O' Level) examination. Students in the Normal Course study either the Normal (Academic) or Normal (Technical) curriculum, which also lasts for four years, leading to the GCE 'N' Level examination. For students in the Normal (Academic) Course who perform well in their GCE 'N' Levels examination, they will study one more year before taking part in the GCE 'O' Level examination. As part of a well-rounded education, secondary students are required to participate in at least one of the many co-curricular activities (CCAs) offered by their schools. Such CCAs include sports, arts, and uniformed groups (student groups who wear a group uniform and participate in activities that promote teamwork and discipline). Such activities, which are a

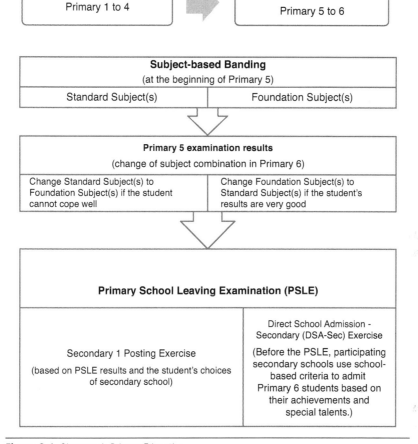

Figure 2.1 Singapore's Primary Education

critical part of holistic education, serve to inculcate qualities of confidence, adaptability and resilience in students. CCA performance can be considered for school admission in the next phase of a student's education.

After completing four or five years of secondary school education, students will participate in the GCE 'O' Level examination. Those whose 'O' Level results are good enough to carry on academic education can opt to apply for admission to junior colleges and polytechnics. Junior colleges offer a curriculum that prepares students for tertiary education at universities. These students sit for the GCE 'A' Level

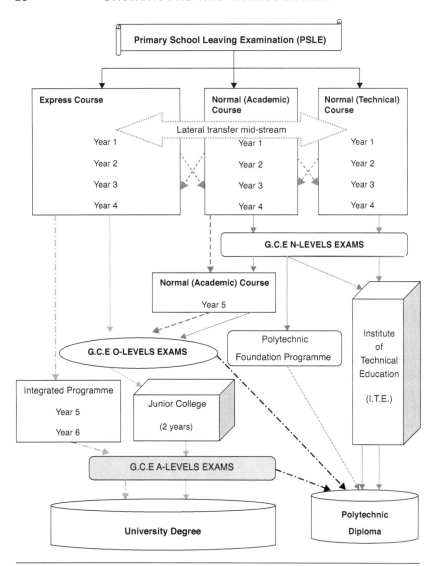

Figure 2.2 Singapore's Secondary Education

examination at the end of a two-year programme. Polytechnics, on the other hand, offer a three-year programme which prepares students for direct entry into the workforce. Some polytechnic students, who obtain very good results at the end of their polytechnic education, can apply for admission into universities.

Most secondary students complete the GCE 'O' Level examination before they proceed with their post-secondary education. However, some students who are academically strong are allowed to proceed to junior college education without taking the GCE 'O' Level if they are admitted to the Integrated Programme (IP). IP was implemented by the MOE in 2004 in selected schools to develop academically strong students both in academic and non-academic curricula. Instead of preparing for the GCE 'O' Level examinations, these students use the time to engage in an enriched curriculum. IP schools use school-based assessments to monitor students' performance before they take the GCE 'A' Level examinations in their final year.

For the students from the Normal (Technical) Course, they can apply to the Institute of Technical Education (ITE) after they have completed the GCE 'N' Level examination. ITE education caters to students who show an aptitude for hands-on learning to further develop their talents and skills through industry-relevant one- or two-year courses and various industry internships. Polytechnics and ITEs have established links to specific industrial sectors over the years and provide practical learning applicable to the workplace. Increasingly, their graduates are sought out by employers.

Phases of Development of the Singapore Education System

The Singapore education system went through a few phases of development from the 1960s. The emphasis of education shifted according to developing situations in the social, political and economic and technological spheres, both locally and globally. There are three phases of development:[9]

- Phase of standardisation (mid-1960s to mid-1980s)
- Phase of local accountability (mid-1980s to mid-1990s)
- Phase of diversity and innovation (mid-1990s to today)

Singapore started with a phase of standardisation from the mid-1960s to mid-1980s. At the start of this phase, the main challenge for Singapore was to survive. During those days, the people were poor and there was severe unemployment. The economy was based primarily on port and warehousing activities, which could hardly sustain the country.

There was a need to expand the industrial base, attract foreign manufacturers, provide jobs and start an export economy. But Singaporeans were mostly illiterate and unskilled. There were major weaknesses in the education system. Schools had low standards, ineffective curriculum and inefficient organisation. The focus of this difficult period was on expanding basic education quickly to supply labour for industrialisation. To ensure a basic level of quality in schooling, the different schools that had been established by the various ethnic or religious groups were absorbed into a single education system, managed and funded by the government. New schools were built. The government introduced the bilingual policy so that all children would learn English as their working language and their own mother tongues. English was used as the medium of instruction for mathematics and science. The quality of education was quite low then. In the early 1970s, out of a cohort of children entering Primary 1, only 35% gained three or more O-level examination passes after 10 years of schooling.

The government conducted a system-wide review of education in the late 1970s, and this effort culminated in the watershed 1979 Goh Report.[10] The report highlighted problems such as large numbers of premature school leavers, high failure rates in national examinations, and low literacy levels among school leavers. Other issues that were emphasised included the unevenness of the quality of schooling and a lack of professional management of the schools.[11] Following the recommendations of this report, streaming was introduced at the end of Primary 3 and at the start of Secondary 1. The reasoning was that students did not learn at the same pace and that streaming would allow students to learn at a rate more suitable for them. It was also considered easier for teachers to instruct a class where students were progressing at a similar pace. Significant reforms were implemented in the areas of school management, curriculum and general work flow. To ensure a baseline standard in schools, a prescribed performance model was applied to them. School appraisal conducted by a team of inspectors from the education ministry was introduced in 1980. The education system was centralised and standardised to support nation building and industrialisation.[12] The government exerted firm control on the schools to implement its national agenda. Centralisation and standardisation at that time were matters of strategic necessity.

The education system shifted to a phase of local accountability in the mid-1980s to mid-1990s.[13] One of the triggers for the shift was the 1985 global economic crisis. The crisis hit Singapore hard. It showed clearly and painfully that while Singapore has successfully built an industrial economy, the strategy was no longer tenable in the long run. In order to survive economically, Singapore had to develop high value-adding technology and service industries. This strategy was articulated in the 1986 Economic Committee Report.[14] Consequently, education had to be revamped to support the new economic strategy. The standardised education system developed during the previous phase was found to be inadequate for the 1990s.

During the phase of local accountability, the focus was to improve educational efficiency and effectiveness by shifting some powers, responsibilities and accountability from headquarters to the schools. Education was reformed to support the country's move from a labour-intensive economy to a capital and skill-intensive one. Although the system was still predominantly a centralised one, signs of decentralisation began to show. Schools were given more autonomy in curricula and pedagogical matters but were held accountable for the results. In 1986, a few high-achieving schools were granted 'independent' status. They were given the freedom to hire and fire school leaders and teachers, undertake financial projects, set school fees and decide student admission policies. Most schools today still do not decide on such matters but follow a common set of guidelines from the MOE. A very significant event during this phase was the introduction of school ranking in 1992. League tables were published in the newspapers. The reasoning was that if schools competed among themselves, they would improve. Also, parents and students were given the ranking information to make informed choices. Competition among schools started to heat up. Schools began to find ways to differentiate and market themselves.

The current phase of diversity and innovation, which began in the mid-1990s, continues the move to give more autonomy to schools, albeit within a framework of adherence to national policies and quality assurance mechanisms. I call this paradox 'centralised decentralisation' and will discuss it in Chapter 5. Although the previous phase of education development had produced fruitful results, it again became painfully clear during the 1997 Asian financial crisis that the world was shifting towards a global knowledge economy and Singapore had to change. The rules of competition among nations were redefined. The competitive edge would increasingly be determined by creativity and innovation. However, through the previous phases, the education system had grown used to a level of conformity to standards.[15] There was much reliance on instructions from headquarters and external appraisal. The formula that had led to success in the 1980s was now a recipe for disaster going into the 21st century. There was then an urgent need to improve the innovative capacity of the nation and to create more educational pathways for young people. A paradigm shift in Singapore's education system was required. This ushered in the phase of diversity and innovation.

Signaling the start of this new phase was the launch of a national vision called Thinking Schools, Learning Nation (TSLN) in 1997. Introduced by Goh Chok Tong, who was then prime minister, TSLN was a vision for a total learning environment in the country. Thinking Schools envisaged a school system that could develop creative thinking skills, lifelong learning passion and nationalistic commitment in young people. Learning Nation envisaged learning as a national culture, allowing creativity and innovation to flourish in the entire society.[16] TSLN emerged from a strategic review of education, motivated by the need to address the challenges of technological advancement, increased competition and globalisation. It guided the system-wide education initiatives that followed subsequently. In particular, National Education (NE), launched in 1997, aimed to develop national cohesion in young people. The five-year Information Technology (IT) Masterplan in Education (subsequently labeled as Masterplan 1) was also launched in 1997 and aimed at creating a technology enabled learning environment in every school. (Singapore is currently implementing Masterplan 4.) The system moved to emphasise the development of creativity, innovation and an enterprising spirit. Students are now more engaged in real world projects and learn to tackle higher order thinking questions.

Many structural changes were made in the system to foster diversity and innovation. In particular, the school cluster system was introduced in 1997 to promote sharing among schools. Cluster Superintendents, who were successful principals, mentored the principals to exercise their enhanced autonomy to undertake school-based reform. In 2000, the inspectorate system was abolished and replaced with a school self-appraisal system, called the School Excellence Model.[17] Schools now set their own goals and annually assess their progress towards them. The results are validated once every five years by an external team. School ranking was replaced by school banding in 2004 and abolished in 2012 to emphasise holistic education.

In 2005, the MOE introduced 'Teach Less, Learn More' (TLLM) to engage students more deeply in learning by transforming curriculum and pedagogy. (TLLM will be further discussed in Chapter 6.) Despite its success, Singapore saw its young learners as overloaded with content, driven to study, but not inspired to do so. TLLM is actually a statement of affirmation from the MOE to shift the focus of education from quantity to quality.[18] Over the next decade, a number of initiatives were launched to improve the quality of education across all levels. For example, in 2009 and 2010 respectively, the Primary Education Review and Implementation (PERI) Committee[19] and the Secondary Education Review and Implementation (SERI) Committee[20] reviewed existing primary and secondary education for quality improvements in the long term. Recommendations from these two review committees shaped and guided several reform initiatives to address students' learning needs and teachers' professional development. Learning spaces were redesigned to support single-session classes and more types of activities in primary schools. New pathways for secondary students were also introduced to accommodate diverse student needs, academic abilities and aptitude.

In 2014, the MOE adopted a framework for 21st century competencies and student outcomes.[21] This framework brings into focus previous efforts at developing a more holistic approach to education so that students can be equipped with life-ready competencies like creativity, innovation, cross-cultural understanding and resilience. In 2015, the broadening of education takes the form of SkillsFuture, a movement that promotes lifelong learning (starting in school) and encourages the deepening of skills during one's adult life (a theme that will be further discussed in Chapter 3).

Conclusion

Although the development of the Singapore education system has been described using three phases for simplicity and clarity, the actual evolutionary process is of course more complex. The phases do not separate historical developments or the type of dynamics clinically. In real life, the Singapore education system displays characteristics of different phases at the same time, although some characteristics are more prominent than others.

Had this book been written a few decades ago, the task of describing the Singapore education system would have been easier. It was easy to describe the pathways then. For example, in the secondary school, students could only follow three major pathways, each of which is determined by their PSLE results, with little option to change pathways in between. These efforts, especially in recent years, have tremendous impact in diversifying the system and increasing the number of pathways for the students. The DSA and IP are good examples of alternative pathways linking one part of the system to another. In the process, Singapore has created a much 'messier' system for itself to manage.

The Singapore education system is changing to keep up with the times. But it takes courage and wisdom to do so. This is a theme that will be discussed in the next chapter.

References

1 Vogel, E. F. (2011). *Deng Xiaoping and the Transformation of China*. Cambridge, MA: Belknap Press of Harvard University Press.
2 Department of Statistics Singapore (2015). *Yearbook of Statistics Singapore*. Singapore: Department of Statistics. (One can also access such publicly available statistics at http://www.singstat.gov.sg)
3 Department of Statistics Singapore (2015). *Yearbook of Statistics Singapore*. Singapore: Department of Statistics.
4 Ministry of Education, Singapore. Retrieved from https://www.moe.gov.sg/
5 Hargreaves, A., Shirley, D., & Ng, P. T. (2012). Singapore: Innovation, communication, and paradox. In A. Hargreaves & D. Shirley, *The Global Fourth Way: The Quest for Educational Excellence* (pp. 71–91). Thousand Oaks, CA: Corwin.
6 Ng, P. T. (2016). Whole systems approach: Professional capital in Singapore. In J. Evers & R. Kneyber (Eds.), *Flip the System: Changing Education from the Ground Up* (pp. 151–158). New York: Routledge.

7 Heng, S. K. (2013, October 21). Government Expenditure on Education. Parliamentary Replies. Retrieved from http://www.moe.gov.sg/media/parliamentary-replies/2013/10/government-expenditure-on-education.php

8 Ministry of Education (MOE) (2015). *For Primary Schools: Subject-Based Banding: Catering to Your Child's Abilities*. Singapore: MOE Communications and Engagement Group. Retrieved from http://www.moe.gov.sg/education/primary/files/subject-based-banding.pdf

9 Ng, P. T. (2008). Quality assurance in the Singapore education system: Phases and paradoxes. *Quality Assurance in Education*, 16(2), 112–125; Ng, P. T. (2010). The evolution and nature of school accountability in the Singapore education system. *Educational Assessment, Evaluation and Accountability*, 22(4), 275–292.

10 Goh, K. S. & Education Study Team (1979). *Report on the Ministry of Education 1978*. Singapore: Singapore National Printers.

11 Wee, H. T. & Chong, K. C. (1990). 25 years of school management. In J. Yip & W. K. Sim (Eds.), *Evolution of Educational Excellence: 25 Years of Education in the Republic of Singapore* (pp. 31–58). Singapore: Longman.

12 Sharpe, L. & Gopinathan, S. (1996). Effective island, effective schools: Repairing and restructuring in the Singapore school system. *International Journal of Educational Reform*, 5(4), 394–402.

13 Ng, P. T. (2008). Quality assurance in the Singapore education system: Phases and paradoxes. *Quality Assurance in Education*, 16(2), 112–125; Ng, P. T. (2010). The evolution and nature of school accountability in the Singapore education system. *Educational Assessment, Evaluation and Accountability*, 22(4), 275–292.

14 Economic Committee (1986). *The Singapore Economy: New Directions*. Singapore: Ministry of Trade and Industry.

15 Ng, P. T. (2008). Quality assurance in the Singapore education system: Phases and paradoxes. *Quality Assurance in Education*, 16(2), 112–125.

16 Goh, C. T. (1997, June 2). *Shaping Our Future: Thinking Schools, Learning Nation*. Speech by Prime Minister Goh Chok Tong at the Opening of the 7th International Conference on Thinking, Suntec City Convention Centre Ballroom. Retrieved from http://www.moe.gov.sg/media/speeches/1997/020697.htm

17 Ng, P. T. (2003). The Singapore school and the school excellence model. *Educational Research for Policy and Practice*, 2(1), 27–39.

18 Ng, P. T. (2008). Educational reform in Singapore: From quantity to quality. *Educational Research for Policy and Practice*, 7(1), 5–15.

19 Ministry of Education (MOE) (2009, April 19). Government Accepts Recommendations on Primary Education—Changes to be Implemented Progressively Over the Next Few Years. Press Release. Retrieved from http://www.moe.gov.sg/media/press/2009/04/government-accepts-recommendat.php

20 Ministry of Education (MOE) (2010, December 28). Strengthening Social-Emotional Support for Secondary School Students—Release of Secondary Education Review and Implementation (SERI) Committee's Report. Press

Release. Retrieved from http://www.moe.gov.sg/media/press/2010/12/
strengthening-social-emotional-support-secondary-school-students.php

21 Ministry of Education (MOE) (2014, April 1). Information Sheet on 21st
Century Competencies. Press Release. Retrieved from http://www.moe.
gov.sg/media/press/2014/04/information-sheet-on-21st-century.php

II

THE FOUR PARADOXES

3

PARADOX 1
Timely Change, Timeless Constants

> Singapore recognises that the recipe for success in the past is a ticket to doom in the future.

If you visit Singapore and talk with some teachers, you will probably hear them say the education system is always changing. Yet, in the same breath, they will also likely say that certain things just do not change at all (sometimes in exasperation)! They have unwittingly articulated a paradox of Singapore. Singapore is a land of change. It is also a land of constants. Singapore is always looking for timely change. It is also hanging on dearly to some timeless constants. Singapore is a land where change and continuity coexist and are equally valued.

Timely Change

Positioned at the top of global education rankings, the Singapore education system is widely seen to be successful by those standards. It has presumably found the recipe for success. Others have come to the island to learn its 'secret'. Singapore has developed a reputation for a packed curriculum, didactic classroom teaching and rote learning. But if these were the features of the education system that have gotten it its stellar international rankings, Singapore seems to be abandoning them. Whatever the recipe for success was, Singapore appears to be discarding it.

Singapore is reforming its education system. Values, innovation, student-centredness, holistic education—these are the new catchphrases. But why does the education system need to change continuously, especially when it is so successful? Why abandon the recipe for success? That reminds me of Sir Humphrey Appleby, the senior civil servant, in the satirical book *Yes, Prime Minister*, who commented that one would not kick away the ladder one climbed up on, especially when one was still standing on it. He was of course referring to British politicians. He meant to say that politicians would not be so 'courageous' to abandon the strategy that has brought them success—not while they were still in power. Common sense, isn't it? But Singapore seems to be kicking away the ladder that it has climbed up on while it is still on that ladder. The question is why.

Why Change?

The global economy that Singapore now participates in is driven by new technologies, business concepts and value propositions. Globalisation has shortened the distance between nations and cities. Technology is creating new businesses and destroying others. Times have changed. A quotable quote is now a tweetable tweet. Singapore can only continue to generate wealth if it can create and exploit knowledge, pursue new technologies and offer high level services. Singapore is a country that survives economically by doing business with the world. It has to adapt to changing global situations. Given its small size, it has to be in touch with global trends and stay ahead of the competition.

Singapore has done well economically for the past five decades. However, past successes do not guarantee future ones. Competition from emerging economies, such as China, India and Vietnam, is heating up. Prime Minister Lee Hsien Loong was understandably concerned:[1]

> China and India alone have one billion workers altogether. Every year, millions of new graduates are entering the workforce. . . seven million [per year] from China . . . [and] if we add in some more from India, it is ten million a year, all hungry, looking for work. Quite formidable.

Formidable indeed, considering that the number of new graduates in big countries is larger than the entire population of Singapore.

The challenge is heightened by rising costs in Singapore, which is a characteristic of maturing cities. Singapore's robust economic fundamentals have attracted higher investments and capital inflows, pushing up the Singapore dollar. In 2015, the Economist Intelligence Unit (EIU) named Singapore as the world's most expensive city.[2] Land and property are expensive. The cost of owning a car is significant, as the government tries to control traffic in the congested city. (It can cost you more than $100,000 US dollars just to put a new Japanese two-litre sedan on the road.) Labour costs are high. Given that human resources are the only resource that Singapore has, Singapore needs a higher value proposition from its people to remain competitive. There is a need to change the nature of education in Singapore in a more fundamental way to create that higher value proposition. As Tharman Shanmugaratnam, who was Education Minister from 2003 to 2008, said:[3]

> We have a strong and robust education system. It is a system well recognized for the high levels of achievement of our students, in all the courses we offer. Our students aim high, and do well by most international comparisons. In recent years we have begun repositioning our education system to help our young meet the challenges of a more competitive and rapidly changing future ... Education has to evolve. We have to prepare for the workplace of the future, which will be very different from the past. If we think we are doing all we need to do because it has worked in the past, we will be blindsided by the changes happening around us.

Heng Swee Keat, who was Education Minister from 2011 to 2015, echoed these ideas:[4]

> Many of the things we do today are good. But let us not keep good in the way of the better. If we keep all the good things, we cannot make way for the better things.

Thus Singapore has to kick away the ladder that got it to where it is now, while still standing on that ladder. It has to abandon its obsession with learning for examinations. It is now focusing on learning for life, embracing holistic education, and developing its young people to think critically and creatively. Singapore is now jumping to another ladder that can take the country further.

It is important to recognise the philosophy here. Singapore changes when it is still successful. One should not wait until one has a problem before one is forced to change. One changes before one has a problem. This is the essence of timely change. Timely change occurs in anticipation of the future. It is change launched from a position of strength rather than one of desperation. But it takes courage to change when one is successful. People around may not wish to change. Why change when the old formula has brought about so much success? Thus the change process in Singapore involves debates, persuasion and nudges. The system evolves surely but sometimes messily. It does not transform clinically or by magic.

Although 'kicking the ladder while standing on it' is a colourful way of expressing the spirit of change, it does not mean the system goes into a free-fall. Rather, the change is a carefully calculated risk, with well thought-through transit plans to shift the system from one state to another. Therefore, timely change requires wisdom as well. In a game of 'chutes and ladders', it is important to jump onto the next ladder, but not a chute that will cause the system to slide. Singapore was successful. But it recognises that the recipe for success in the past is a ticket to doom in the future. It has to reinvent itself in a way that is paradoxically both bold and careful.

In this area, Singapore has a crucial strength. Change is actually part of Singapore's psyche. It is the central theme of the Singapore story. Founding Prime Minister Lee Kuan Yew said in 1967:[5]

> Change is the very essence of life. The moment we cease to change, to be able to adapt, to adjust, to respond effectively to new situations, then we have begun to die.

Since independence, Singapore has understood that standing still was a ticket to doom. It was preoccupied with survival and focused on the future. Through the tough days of nation building, the relentless pursuit of reinventing itself against the odds has become embedded in the national psyche. Lee Kuan Yew spoke in 1969:[6]

> It is the future that counts. We have to make the effort, to plan, to organise, so as to bring into being a more secure, more stable and more prosperous Singapore . . . Fortunately, the present generation has the courage to face

difficult situations. So we have Singapore, making it possible for us to organise ourselves to preserve and safeguard the values that we all cherish.

The same spirit has been present throughout Singapore's history. In the late 1990s, Prime Minister Goh Chok Tong echoed it when faced with the Asian economic crisis:[7]

> We have gone through difficult times before: Confrontation in the 1960s, the British withdrawal in the early 1970s, and the severe recession in 1985. These crises have prepared us, as a nation, for the trials we face today. In time, how we surmount this regional crisis will become another chapter of the Singapore Story . . . We must do nothing to compromise our long term competitiveness, nor be rattled into taking unwise actions under pressure . . . But we need to organise ourselves to weather the storm, and use this period to gain a head start for the race ahead after the storm has subsided.

In the words of current Prime Minister Lee Hsien Loong:[8]

> We worry all the time. People say we are paranoid, which I suppose we are and we need to be . . . Is it to be expected that a population of three-and-a-half million citizens and maybe a million foreign workers will have the best airline in the world? The best airport in the world? One of the busiest ports in the world? . . . It is an entirely unnatural state of affairs . . .

Indeed, it was unnatural and still is. Singapore's success comes not from the endowment of land or natural resources, but from the labours of tenacious and hard-working people. The nation emerged through a sudden baptism of fire. It matured through a long-suffering journey of change. But given that Singapore is now one of the top countries in international rankings, what is it still trying to change? Let me share with you examples from a few significant areas in our recent history.

From Quantity to Quality

While the Singapore education system may be recognised worldwide for its academic rigour and commitment to excellence, the education paradigm is shifting from a focus on quantity to a focus on quality. Simply acing examinations does not equip one for life! Curriculum and pedagogy must be changed so that students are truly engaged in the learning process where higher order thinking skills are honed. This is a century where people are digital natives and information (and misinformation) is easily available. Adaptability to change is going to serve one better and longer than paper qualification.

As part of the effort to focus on quality education, rather than examination results, the MOE launched in 2014 its framework of 21st century competencies to guide the development of education.[9] This framework is a holistic approach to prepare students for future economies and society. Centred on a set of cores values—respect, responsibility, integrity, care, resilience, and harmony—the framework emphasises social and emotional competencies—self-awareness, self-management, social awareness, relationship management, and responsible decision-making. These form the foundation for children and young people to manage themselves and relate with others. To live in the globalised world, the following 21st century skills are necessary:

- Civic literacy, global awareness and cross-cultural skills
- Critical and inventive thinking
- Communication, collaboration and information skills

It is envisaged that every student who graduates from the Singapore school system will be a self-directed learner, a confident person, an active contributor, and a concerned citizen.

But one of the key hurdles to achieving holistic education is the obsession with examination results and getting children into elite schools, on the assumption that these factors ensure a good future. Singapore has made a few bold moves in this area. School ranking, which was instituted in 1992, was replaced by school banding in 2004 and abolished in 2012 to emphasise holistic education. The strategy, which used to be a key lever for school improvement, has outlived its usefulness and was finally scrapped. In 2013, Prime Minister Lee Hsien Loong announced that the PSLE scoring system would change from absolute points to wider grade bands. He said:[10]

> One-point difference in the PSLE scores, 230 versus 231, may make all the difference in your secondary school posting. But at the age of 12, one examination, four papers and you want to measure the child to so many decimal points and say well, this one got one point better than that child? It is a distinction which is meaningless and too fine to make.

Prime Minister Lee reasoned that in doing so, students would not need to chase after the last decimal point. This would reduce excessive competition and stress among students. Teachers would also have the space to educate and develop the students more holistically. Singapore has slaughtered a few sacred cows in its own backyard.

The tertiary sector is also taking bold steps toward change. In 2014, the National University of Singapore (NUS) made a move to curb obsession with grades by implementing a 'grade-free' system for some modules. In this system, students will just be given a distinction, pass, or fail, in their modules instead of receiving the conventional A to F grades for their academic performance. The assessment will not form part of their Cumulative Average Point. The new system encourages students to explore courses that will make their education more holistic and develop qualities that go beyond their main subject areas.[11] Nanyang Technological University (NTU), the world's best young university (under 50 years old), allowed its students in 2014 to earn credits upon successful completion of online courses on the Coursera platform.[12] In the next few years, NTU students will be given the option of completing a maximum of five elective modules online, so that they can skip a semester and even have an earlier graduation. With this saving of time, students are encouraged to select another course or take up research or work attachments.

High performance in international tests may be a good indicator of the quality of the education system for some countries. But Singapore has a different interpretation. The quality that it is aiming for is beyond test scores. It is moving away from a focus on standardised test results to embrace a broader view of educational success. Singapore recognises that the younger generation will need more than high test scores to secure a good future and demonstrates that despite the global recognition it receives for its excellent international league standings, it is able to look beyond those accolades. It continuously evaluates and calibrates its policies in order to keep its education system relevant to the times.

Diversifying Educational Pathways

The current education system, which was described in Chapter 2, has emerged after many changes have taken place throughout the years to loosen what used to be a rigid system many years ago. Singapore has a system of national examinations (ages 12, 16 and 18) that has served it well in many ways. Despite its pressurising effects, the national examination system served as quality control points and determined educational pathways for young people. One had to go through an examination at the end of each stage before progressing to the next. It was neat and systematic. But as the years progressed, some 'bright' students were stifled by the rigid system. Others who were not academically inclined fell through the cracks. One joke in Singapore was that Einstein would not have made it through Singapore's education system. It was a landscape of high plateaus but not many peaks. Thus there was an increasing need to loosen up this educational structure to create diverse pathways for different types of students to progress. An example of a significant change is the Integrated Programme (IP).

When the IP was introduced in 2008, high performing secondary school students in the programme were no longer required to take the GCE 'O' level examinations. Rather, they were placed on a 'through train' to the GCE 'A' level examinations or the International Baccalaureate (IB) after six years of secondary education. Without the 'O' level examinations, the IP allows the students to have more time and flexibility to engage in a broad-based education. They also enjoy more freedom in choosing their subjects of study.

This direction of change is not only for the high performing students. In 2005, the MOE introduced greater flexibility for Normal (Academic) students. Selected Normal (Academic) students who perform well in their school examinations at the end of Secondary 2 or Secondary 3 are able to skip the GCE 'N' level examination at the end of Secondary 4. Instead, they take the GCE 'O' Level examination at the end of Secondary 5.[13] Today, Secondary 4 Normal (Academic) students who perform well in their GCE 'N' Level examination may be able to gain entry to polytechnics through either a one-year Polytechnic Foundation Programme (PFP) at the polytechnics, or a two-year Direct-Entry-Scheme to Polytechnic Programme (DPP) at the ITE.[14]

In 2014, the MOE also introduced greater flexibility in subject offerings at lower secondary levels in 12 secondary schools. All secondary schools will eventually offer this flexibility by 2018. The aim is to allow students to find a better match between their strengths in individual subjects and their subject offerings. For example, students who scored an 'A' for mathematics at the PSLE, regardless of whether they are in the Normal (Academic) or Normal (Technical) course, will be given a chance to study mathematics at the Express level in Secondary 1.[15] In a way, such flexibility is a signal that the PSLE no longer has the final word on the academic pathway of a student in the secondary school.

Although Singapore's education system is known globally to have a strong emphasis on mathematics and science, it is branching out to emphasise more areas of learning and success.[16] For example, specialised schools, such as the Singapore Sports School (SSS) and School of the Arts (SOTA) were set up in 2004 and 2008, respectively. SSS incorporates sports training within a four-year secondary education. Students learn to balance sports training with academic lessons in their daily schedule. SOTA exposes students to issues and practices in the arts industry and allows students time and space for artistic practice and training. They are also required to take up internships with a professional arts company, which prepares them for admission into arts institutes and conservatories both locally and internationally. It offers students a choice between a more academically rigorous International Baccalaureate (IB) diploma programme and a more career-centric IB career-related certificate programme. These specialised schools add diversity to the education landscape. They provide opportunities for success to students whose are gifted in sports and arts, rather than mathematics and science.

Lifelong Learning and SkillsFuture

Singapore is also changing its mindset that learning takes place only in schools. In August 2014, the prime minister announced that in the future, Singapore would make both the school and the workplace twin sites of learning, as learners upgraded themselves continuously throughout life. This SkillsFuture movement is specifically geared to promoting a culture of lifelong learning in the country and encouraging the acquisition of deep skills throughout working life.[17] It is a national effort to shift the focus on academic performance as the measure for success towards mastery of deep but practical skills that are relevant to every working adult Singaporean. The initiative provides support for skills mastery for every Singaporean, regardless of their academic qualification. It involves multiple stakeholders and strengthens the school-industry-community link, with the government acting in a facilitative role. It carries a message that whether in school or at work, there are more ways to succeed in life than having the right paper qualifications. Rather, one has to be good at what one is doing and embrace an attitude of always trying to do better by enhancing one's knowledge, application and experience. Current Education Minister (Higher Education and Skills) Ong Ye Kung said:[18]

> Study and work will no longer be sequential, but interspersed with each other throughout a person's life. We are moving from education as a concept of flow, i.e. preparing young students to enter the workforce, to a concept of stock, i.e. helping everyone in society learn throughout their lives. More fundamentally, and over time, we should blur the differentiation between PET (pre-employment training) and CET (continuing education and training . . . if we succeed in our effort, we will have a better balance between knowledge and skills pursuits, between academic and competency accomplishments, and across a wide spectrum of disciplines that is more reflective of the needs of the economy and personal aspirations.

SkillsFuture is uncharted territory in Singapore's history. It requires this generation to be pioneers again. It calls for a shift in the mindset about education among Singaporeans. Current strategies in the implementation of SkillsFuture hinge upon the idea of linking training and education with industry needs by developing courses and training options that are meaningful to Singaporeans. These measures are meant to broaden paths to success in life so that conventional academic attainment will not be the only (and overcrowded) path in Singapore.

In developing this scheme, Singapore studied the example of apprenticeship programmes in Switzerland and Germany. As part of SkillsFuture, enhanced internships will be offered to students so that they can learn through meaningful work assignments and exposure to industry. These internships will also help students deepen and apply both technical and soft skills, and make better career choices through real world exposure to various industries. Under the Young Talent

Programme (YTP), overseas immersion is extended to polytechnic and ITE students, not just university students. They can sign up for overseas internships to prepare them to take on international assignments in their careers. In 2016, the government opened a SkillsFuture Credit account for every citizen aged 25 years and above, with an opening credit of S$500 to support his or her learning needs at any time. The credit can be used to pay for work-skills related courses. Periodic top-ups to the account will be made by the government. These are some examples of the wide range of initiatives under SkillsFuture.[19]

Had Singapore simply wanted to keep its reputation by maintaining its excellent results in the international leagues tables, it would have doubled its efforts in mathematics and science for students at the age of 15 to get them ready for PISA. Instead, Singapore is actively changing its education system. The responsibility of the education system is to develop children and young people holistically to prepare them for their future. Education is not a game of international league tables.

I have often been asked: Is PISA important to Singapore? My response is 'yes' and 'no'! In Singapore, PISA is one of the few recognised international comparison tests that we use to benchmark where we are in the world. This provides an indication (but not an absolute measure) of our current and future global competitiveness. Therefore, PISA results and findings are useful. But Singapore's position in the PISA league table is not the goal—quality education is. PISA does not tell us whether our students are holistically developed or otherwise. So, while PISA is a useful reference for certain areas of our work, it is not our report card.

Timeless Constants

Change must be timely to adapt to a world that is rapidly changing. But change must also be anchored in something timeless so that one is not lost in the waves of change. In a world where change is the only constant, there are constants that do not and should not change. These timeless constants are Singapore's beacons during change so that the education system will not lose its mission and identity in the waves of change. What are some of these constants?

Firstly, Singapore's philosophy is that education is an investment, not an expenditure. This is because "education is the key to the long term future of any people", as Lee Kuan Yew put it.[20] When money allocated to education is seen as an expenditure, the attitude is to cut costs whenever possible. But when money allocated to education is seen as an investment, one does not begrudge the money at all. One aims only to maximise the return on investment.

This philosophy is not some empty campaign slogan. The country has put its money where its mouth is, and has done so consistently. Lee Kuan Yew, after passing what was considered a big budget for education during a time when Singapore's economy was weak during the tumultuous period in the nation's founding history, said:[21]

> Now, we do not grudge this money but we must get its worth returned to us in good citizens who are robust, well-educated, skilled and well-adjusted people.

In 2001, Goh Chok Tong echoed these thoughts:[22]

> We will spend more on education. We will increase spending from the current 3.6% of our GDP, to 4.5%. This translates to about $1.5 billion more each year, or an additional $2,500 per student. The additional funds will be invested in better facilities, curriculum development, and teachers.

In 2012, Lee Hsien Loong explained Singapore's philosophy regarding the education budget:[23]

> The most important long term investment we can make is in our people and to make it through education. It is the key response to progress in technology and to the changing world.

The 2008–9 global financial crisis put this philosophy to the test. Many countries cut their education budget as part of an austerity response. Singapore did the opposite—something almost unthinkable considering that its economy was badly affected.[24] The education budget was S$8.0 billion before the financial crisis in 2008. This was increased to S$8.7 billion during the crisis in 2009. Tharman Shanmugaratnam, who was then finance minister, declared that the government would not cut back spending on education even in that economic downturn, because[25]

Education is a necessary investment in good times as well as in bad times. In these difficult times, it is even more important for us to invest in the future, so that Singapore, as a country, is ready to take up new challenges when the economy picks up.

Secondly, good teachers are regarded as the key to a good education system. This understanding has not changed throughout the years. Lee Kuan Yew said in 1966 that[26]

> just as a country is as good as its citizens, so its citizens are, really, only as good as their teachers.

Goh Chok Tong returned to this subject of quality teachers in 2001:[27]

> Teachers are the heart and soul of education. We can sink all our money into physical infrastructure and curriculum, but without good teachers, these investments will not pay off. The quality of education our young receive depends on the quality of our teachers. Our past achievements would not have been possible without our teachers. Our future achievements will depend on them.

In 2015, Heng Swee Keat continued in the same vein:[28]

> Teachers play a central role in nation-building. Together, you are part of something much bigger—in spirit and in purpose, in mission and in heart. The little successes you experience in every classroom accumulate to contribute to the huge steps we take as a nation. The young people you teach will be the pioneers of SG100 (100th anniversary of Singapore's independence). Through your collective hands, you will raise the generation that will take Singapore forward in the next 50 years.

Singapore is one of the few countries in the world that really value and build the teaching profession, in word and deed. It designs differentiated career tracks for teachers and invests heavily in their professional development. It pays teachers a salary that is competitive in the labour market. It does everything to make teaching a respectable and respected profession.

Thirdly, Singapore understands the importance of character and citizenship education. Whether through the Education for Living (EFL) programme in 1979, Civic and Moral Education in 1991, or National Education in 1997, the education system has consistently performed its role in inculcating moral values and desirable social attitudes in the young so as to nurture them into becoming good people and loyal citizens. Lee Kuan Yew said in 1967 that schools would have to teach students social norms of good and bad, and to distinguish right and wrong, because "without these values, a literate generation may be more dangerous than a completely uneducated one".[29]

In the context of a fragile multicultural society, it is important for the education system to carry messages such as racial and religious harmony, consensus not conflict, national cohesion, the instinct for survival and confidence in the future. In 2015, Heng Swee Keat addressed teachers with these thoughts in mind:[30]

> Singapore's stability and growth is not something we can take for granted. Understand Singapore's challenges and opportunities. Constantly ask yourselves what these all mean for how you prepare our students for the future, how you nurture in them a sense of citizenship and nationhood. Your classrooms are where your students begin to appreciate how exceptional our Singapore story is, and how much work went into beating the odds. So I urge you to bring these lessons into your classrooms, because this is about everyone's future.

Today, character and citizenship education (CCE) in Singapore adopts a whole-school approach. It is integrated with the schools' academic and co-curricular activities (CCA) platform. CCE addresses the need for social cohesion in a multicultural society and a sense of rootedness to Singapore amidst its rapid globalisation and economic development. CCE also aims to develop good values in the students and their socio-emotional competencies. Current Education Minister (Schools) Ng Chee Meng, in speaking about putting values in action, said:[31]

> To me, this is what education is all about—it's not just about grades, not just about the cognitive development, but the development of the whole being.

Conclusion

Timely change. Timeless constants. Time and again, Singapore has demonstrated its willingness to change and its courage to stick with fundamentals. There is change, and there is continuity. The education system today is not the result of one policy or one minister. It is the result of half a decade of systematic building, upgrading and refurbishing by many ministers, officials, school leaders, teachers and teacher trainers. In 2015, when two new ministers, Ng Chee Meng and Ong Ye Kung, were appointed to the Education Ministry, they released a joint message that they would continue to build on the work of Minister Heng Swee Keat and the past ministers, and the many officials and practitioners who have developed the Singapore education system over generations. They too would like every school to be a good school, every student an engaged learner, every teacher a caring educator and every parent a supportive partner. Thus they will see to the expansion of the system in both scale and complexity, and build more and better pathways for Singaporeans to fulfil their passions and aspirations.[32] This is unlike many other countries where a change in minister implies an upheaval in the education system in terms of policies and practices. In Singapore, slaughtering sacred cows and maintaining continuity come together.

Of course, not every policy in Singapore's history has been 'spot on' or well-received. When Singapore implemented the Graduate Mothers' Scheme in 1984, which gave priority admission to schools to children of graduate mothers, many citizens were not convinced. It was an attempt to get graduates to have more babies. But the scheme was perceived to be divisive and generated fierce debates in the society. It was discontinued in 1985. Timely change does not mean Singapore always gets it right. It is prepared to adjust or discard an idea if the idea is not working.

To talk about timelessness in a country with only half a century of independence seems itself to be quite incredible. But I feel that when change is fast and furious, we have to be even more mindful of what we are really doing. We have to exercise judgement wisely and courageously, and not be seduced by what is popular. Sometimes, it is absolutely necessary to go back to basics. In a world where everyone is constantly and mindlessly changing, those who stand still on fundamentals stand out! We need to stand firm on the basics in order to have a solid platform for change.

Should PISA be a wake-up call to other countries? Perhaps, but every country should always be concerned about its children's education, with or without PISA. If PISA prompts a government to do a serious inquiry into the deep issues in education and find solutions to them, then that is good. But knee-jerk reactions are unhelpful, as are convenient and selective uses and interpretations of PISA results to justify decisions which have already been made. (There is a difference between evidence-based decision-making and decision-based evidence-gathering.) Also, if people get too anxious over PISA, it will be just another rat race. Based on Singapore's experience, if I were in a position to advise governments all over the world, my exhortation would be "Please do not jump to conclusions by a glance at the PISA league tables and please do not turn PISA into a world examination for kids."

Many education systems push for changes that are visible and quick. They may gain popular approval, but they will not provide a firm foundation for long term development. Like the soaring towers in modern Singapore, education systems must build downwards so that they may, with inner strength and confidence, build upwards.

Education is an investment, not an expenditure.

References

1 Lee, H. L. (2013, August 18). Prime Minister Lee Hsien Loong's National Day Rally Speech 2013. Retrieved from http://www.pmo.gov.sg/mediacentre/prime-minister-lee-hsien-loongs-national-day-message-2013-english

2 The Economist Intelligence Unit (2015). Worldwide Cost of Living 2015. Retrieved from http://ifuturo.org/documentacion/WCOL-March.pdf

3 Tharman, S. (2003, October 2). *The Next Phase in Education: Innovation and Enterprise*. Speech by Mr Tharman Shanmugaratnam, Acting Minister for Education, at the Ministry of Education Work Plan Seminar, Singapore. Retrieved from http://www.moe.gov.sg/media/speeches/2003/sp20031002.htm

4 Heng, S. K. (2013, September 25). Keynote Address by Mr Heng Swee Keat, Minister for Education, at the Ministry of Education Work Plan Seminar at the Ngee Ann Polytechnic Convention Centre, Singapore. Retrieved from http://www.moe.gov.sg/media/speeches/2013/09/25/keynote-address-by-mr-heng-swee-keat-at-the-ministry-of-education-work-plan-seminar-2013.php

5 Lee, K. Y. (1967, April 26). Speech by Prime Minister Lee Kuan Yew at the 4th Delegates Conference of the National Trades Union Congress at the Conference Hall, Trade Union House, Singapore. Retrieved from http://www.nas.gov.sg/archivesonline/speeches/record-details/743648df-115d-11e3-83d5-0050568939ad

6 Lee, K. Y. (1969, August 19). Excerpts Of Prime Minister's Speech at Hua Yi Government Chinese Secondary School at the Exhibition Depicting the Progress of Singapore's Education in the last 150 Years, Singapore. Retrieved from http://www.nas.gov.sg/archivesonline/data/pdfdoc/lky 19690819.pdf

7 Goh, C. T. (1998, August 23). Speech by Prime Minister Goh Chok Tong at the National Day Rally. Retrieved from http://www.moe.gov.sg/media/speeches/1998/23aug98.htm

8 Cited in Khamid, H. M. A. & Siong, O. (2015, August 22). PM Lee tackles questions on governance at SG50+ conference. *Channel NewsAsia.* Retrieved from http://www.channelnewsasia.com/news/singapore/pm-lee-tackles-questions/1956798.html

9 Ministry of Education (MOE) (2014, April 1). Information Sheet on 21st Century Competencies. MOE Press Release. Retrieved from http://www.moe.gov.sg/media/press/2014/04/information-sheet-on-21st-century.php

10 Lee, H. L. (2013, August 18). Prime Minister Lee Hsien Loong's National Day Rally Speech 2013. Retrieved from http://www.pmo.gov.sg/mediacentre/prime-minister-lee-hsien-loongs-national-day-message-2013-english

11 Ong, H. H. (2014, January 25). NUS takes a bold move to curb obsession with grades. *The Straits Times*, pp. B1–B2.

12 Davie, S. (2014, November 13). Credit to NTU for its online courses. *The Straits Times*. Retrieved from http://news.asiaone.com/news/education/credit-ntu-its-online-courses

13 Ministry of Education (MOE) (2005, September 22). Greater Flexibility and Choice for Learners. MOE Press Release. Retrieved from https://www.moe.gov.sg/media/press/2005/pr20050922a.htm

14 Ministry of Education (MOE) (2015). For Normal (Academic) Students. Through-Train Pathways: Diverse Pathways to Fulfil Your Potential. Retrieved from http://www.moe.gov.sg/education/post-secondary/files/through-train-pathways-na-students.pdf

15 Ministry of Education (MOE) (2013, November 14). Greater Flexibility in Secondary School Subject Offering. MOE Press Release. Retrieved from http://www.moe.gov.sg/media/press/2013/11/greater-flexibility-in-secondary-school-subject-offering.php

16 Ministry of Education (MOE) (2002, October 15). Government Accepts Recommendations for a Broader and More Flexible Curriculum and a More Diverse JC/Upper Secondary Education Landscape. MOE Press Release. Retrieved from http://www.moe.gov.sg/media/press/2002/pr15102002.htm

17 Ministry of Education (MOE) (2014, November 5). SkillsFuture Council Begins Work: Driving National Effort to Develop Skills for the Future. MOE Press Release. Retrieved from http://www.moe.gov.sg/media/press/2014/11/skillsfuture-council-begins-work.php

18 Ong, Y. K. (2015, October 14). Speech by Mr Ong Ye Kung, Acting Minister for Education (Higher Education and Skills), at the Opening of the OECD-Singapore Conference on Higher Education Futures, Resorts

World Convention Centre, Singapore. Retrieved from http://www.moe.gov.sg/media/speeches/2015/10/14/speech-by-mr-ong-ye-kung-at-the-opening-of-the-oecd-singapore-conference-on-higher-education-futures.php

19 Ministry of Education (MOE) (2015, February 25). SkillsFuture: Skills-Future Credit. Press Release. Retrieved from http://www.moe.gov.sg/media/press/2015/02/skillsfuture-skillsfuture-credit.php

20 Lee, K. Y. (1993, November 8). Speech by Lee Kuan Yew, Senior Minister, for Africa Leadership Forum at the Regent Hotel, Singapore. Retrieved from http://www.nas.gov.sg/archivesonline/data/pdfdoc/lky19931108.pdf

21 Lee, K. Y. (1966, December 27). *Education and Nation-Building*. Transcript of the Prime Minister's Speech at the Opening of the Seminar at the Conference Hall, Singapore. Retrieved from http://www.nas.gov.sg/archivesonline/data/pdfdoc/lky19661227.pdf

22 Goh, C. T. (2001, August 31). *Shaping Lives, Moulding Nation*. Speech by Prime Minister Goh Chok Tong at the Teachers' Day Rally, at the Singapore Expo. Retrieved from http://www.nas.gov.sg/archivesonline/speeches/view-html?filename=2001083103.htm

23 Lee, H. L. (2012). *A Home with Hope and Heart*. Prime Minister Lee Hsien Loong's National Day Rally 2012. Retrieved from http://www.pmo.gov.sg/mediacentre/prime-minister-lee-hsien-loongs-national-day-rally-2012-speech-english

24 Ng, P. T. (2011). Singapore's response to the global war for talent: Politics and education. *International Journal of Educational Development*, 31(3), 262–268.

25 Tharman, S. (2009, January 22). *Keeping Jobs, Building for the Future*. Budget Statement 2009 by Mr Tharman Shanmugaratnam, Finance Minister, at the Parliament, Singapore. Retrieved from http://www.singaporebudget.gov.sg/budget_2009/speech_toc/index.html

26 Lee, K. Y. (1966, December 27). *Education and Nation-Building*. Transcript of the Prime Minister's Speech at the Opening of the Seminar at the Conference Hall, Singapore. Retrieved from http://www.nas.gov.sg/archivesonline/data/pdfdoc/lky19661227.pdf

27 Goh, C. T. (2001, August 31). *Shaping Lives, Moulding Nation*. Speech by Prime Minister Goh Chok Tong at the Teachers' Day Rally, at the Singapore Expo. Retrieved from http://www.nas.gov.sg/archivesonline/speeches/view-html?filename=2001083103.htm

28 Heng, S. K. (2015, July 6). Speech by Mr Heng Swee Keat, Minister for Education, at the NIE Teachers' Investiture Ceremony at the Nanyang Auditorium, Nanyang Technological University, Singapore. Retrieved from http://www.moe.gov.sg/media/speeches/2015/07/06/speech-by-mr-heng-swee-keat-at-the-nie-teachers-investiture-ceremony.php

29 Lee, K. Y. (1967, August 8). Prime Minister's Address on TV on the Eve of National Day. Retrieved from http://www.nas.gov.sg/archivesonline/data/pdfdoc/lky19670808.pdf

30 Heng, S. K. (2015, July 6). Speech by Mr Heng Swee Keat, Minister for Education, at the NIE Teachers' Investiture Ceremony at the Nanyang Auditorium, Nanyang Technological University, Singapore. Retrieved from http://www.moe.gov.sg/media/speeches/2015/07/06/speech-by-mr-heng-swee-keat-at-the-nie-teachers-investiture-ceremony.php

31 Ng, C. M. (2015, October 16). Speech by Mr Ng Chee Meng, Acting Minister for Education (Schools) and Senior Minister of State for Transport, at the NIE Leaders in Education Programme Graduation Dinner, at the Regent Singapore Hotel. Retrieved from http://www.moe.gov.sg/media/speeches/2015/10/16/speech-by-mr-ng-chee-meng-at-the-nie-leaders-in-education-programme-graduation-dinner.php

32 Ng, C. M. & Ong, Y. K. (2015). A Joint Message from Ng Chee Meng, Acting Minister for Education (Schools), and Ong Ye Kung, Acting Minister for Education (Higher Education and Skills). Retrieved from http://www.moe.gov.sg/media/speeches/2015/10/06/a-joint-message-from-acting-ministers-for-education.php

4

PARADOX 2
Compassionate Meritocracy

One of the complaints about Singapore among its residents concerns the 'unforgiving' meritocratic system of examinations and results that glorifies those who excel and stigmatises those who fail along their academic journey. The world is your oyster if you excel. It is the end of the world if you fail. Resources are channeled to groom the top students. Others languish at the bottom. That is one picture. But, if you visit the Ministry of Education, you will hear officials describe the huge efforts put into levelling up students who are struggling in the meritocratic system. Visit an Institute of Technical Education and you will be more impressed with its state-of-the-art campus and facilities than you would be in an 'elite' secondary school. Some might ask, 'But isn't Singapore "religiously" meritocratic and elitist?' Well, Singapore aims to be a compassionate meritocracy.

Meritocracy

Meritocracy is a philosophy that ties power and advancement with individual merit. It is generally understood to be a practice that awards an individual higher social status, job position, income level and general recognition based on merit. The term 'meritocracy' was first coined by Michael Young in a satirical tale called The Rise of the Meritocracy 1870–2033. The tale describes a dystopian future in which one's social place is determined by IQ and effort.[1] It was intended to point out the folly of the concept. However, today, instead of a pejorative term, 'meritocracy' has become a positive ideal in some parts of the world. In fact, the merit of meritocracy is often taken for granted and assumed to be a moral and normative standard to be upheld.

Proponents of meritocracy argue that the practice gives all deserving individuals an equal and fair chance of achieving success on their own merit, which is usually a mixture of effort and talent, rather than on their race or social class.[2] Education and achievements in education often become cornerstones of this meritocracy. Essentially, the argument is that all children should receive the same level of provision in education. By testing them and selecting them on the basis of their test results, a system of social and economic ranking will evolve. Meritocracy is presented as a just and productive method of social progression, allowing for distinctions to be made on the basis of performance.[3] An education system that separates the children of the wealthy and the middle class from those of the poor and from minorities cannot be considered adequate for a democratic society.[4]

However, there are challenges to the practice of meritocracy. A key concern with meritocracy is the lack of a clear definition of 'merit'. Which 'merit' is to be considered merit and what standards need to be reached to be considered as a merit raise questions about the appropriate merits and standards.[5]

Opponents of this concept argue that a particular definition of merit generates a new elitist class which excludes others. As Michael Young argues, 'meritocrats' are encouraged to believe that they have gotten to where they are through their own merits, and they therefore have the moral upper-hand and feelings of righteousness to reward themselves even further, increasing the gap between the haves and have-nots.[6] Successful people can always be justified after the fact as deserving their success based on their merit. This justifies the status quo and consolidates the grip of the successful on more success. The rich become richer while the poor become poorer. Even in schools, modern educational meritocracy, expressed in terms of effort, education and examinations, generates a system where everything is focused on measurable outcomes. Teachers and students are tempted to adopt questionable strategies to help themselves prosper in the system, which act to the detriment of a more holistic educational experience.[7]

Meritocracy in Singapore

Singapore is unarguably and unapologetically a meritocratic society. Since its independence in 1965, meritocracy has been one of its key principles of governance.[8] The country runs a system that promotes able people or those with talent regardless of race, language, religion or family background. Through a highly competitive education system culminating in government scholarships, top positions in the civil service and political leadership are filled by individuals with demonstrated track records of merit as measured by achievements.[9] People from all backgrounds have every chance to rise to the top based on their own merit.

Lee Kuan Yew, who was prime minister from 1965 to 1990, was himself from a non-elite background, although he subsequently graduated from Cambridge University with a law degree. Lee Kuan Yew famously said in 1974 that the main burden of planning and implementing Singapore's strategies at that time rested on the shoulders of some 300 key persons. If all 300 were to crash in one plane, he said Singapore would then disintegrate.[10] His governing belief was that if the country groomed a small group of highly talented people that would lead the rest, this would ultimately benefit the entire population. This small group of talented individuals would work to optimise the well-being of society. Any imperfections in the meritocracy or shortcomings in social mobility would be moderated by constant attention by this talented group to increasing opportunities for others. Lee Kuan Yew therefore promoted a system that provided equality of opportunity, where the people with merit would rise to the top.[11]

The Singapore education system has adhered to the meritocratic principle. In the years following independence, upward social mobility was brought about through meritocracy. When many people were immigrants and working hard for a better life, the notion of non-discrimination by race, language or religion offered hope for outcomes that these immigrants scarcely dreamt of. The hawker's son might become a lawyer. The cleaner's daughter might become a doctor. Some of them really did. In one generation, there was a significant shift of families up the economic ladder in a rapidly expanding society. The meritocratic principle worked.

However, the meritocratic principle offers at best equal opportunities, not outcomes. Today, Singapore is a developed nation and competition is keener than ever before. With an open economy that is highly influenced by global forces, inequality becomes more likely as a consequence. With a larger base of middle class families, upward social mobility becomes much harder. There are also those who fall through the cracks, even given the equality of opportunities.

It is already a great challenge to provide all students with equal opportunities when children come from different backgrounds and go to school differently prepared. Affluent families obviously have ample financial resources to support their children. Those who have less financial means do not have this competitive advantage. The starting line is never exactly the same.[12] To be part of the successful group, many parents and students succumb to the pressure of a highly competitive education system. There is increasing marketisation in Singapore's system,[13] as in many other parts of the world such as the United States and England.[14]

The other side of this argument is expressed in the question raised by Prime Minister Lee Hsien Loong, who asked what the alternative could possibly be if Singapore was not based on meritocracy:[15]

> Because I ask myself, if we are not going on merit, if we are not going to invest in people who are capable, if we are not going to put capable people into important jobs, judging by how able they are doing their job, then how are you going to do it? What are you going to look at? . . . You have a choice—you can look at wealth . . . connections . . . you want that? Some countries do that, but I don't think that's a Singapore you want . . . I believe we must still base our society on merit, but with wide definitions of merit and success.

One area of concern of the Singapore society is that its score on indices of economic inequality is high (Gini indices of 0.478 in 2012, 0.463 in 2013, 0.464 in 2014), with higher earners moving ahead faster than low-wage workers. There is intense public and media debate about the merits and drawbacks of meritocracy[16] because meritocracy is one of the national governing philosophies that have been commonly invoked to emphasise the merit of the socio-political system. Singaporeans, who are unhappy with actual and perceived inequality and with limited social mobility, blame the principle of meritocracy for their situation. This raises the question of how Singapore should cope with the conundrum first posed by Michael Young in *The Rise of the Meritocracy*.[17] What will a society do when those in its 'lowest rungs' finally come to grasp that, having been given every opportunity, their status and reward are simply all that they could achieve, given their 'merit'?

'Compassionate Meritocracy': No Child Held Back; No Child Left Behind

Meritocracy will remain in Singapore, at least for the foreseeable future. But it cannot stay as it is. The problem of the increasing wealth gap among people does not mean that the meritocratic principle is no longer applicable. But this does suggest that the nature of the meritocracy has to change with the times. In particular, in the education system, how does Singapore reconcile its 'ruthless' meritocratic system with its desire to help every child succeed?

One response to this challenge has been the paradoxical philosophy of 'compassionate meritocracy', a term coined by Goh Chok Tong in 2013:[18]

> We do not want a society whose citizens seek to advance their own interests without a care for others, or worse, at the expense of others. I call this 'selfish meritocracy' . . . It is up to those of us who can, to reach back and help those behind to climb the ladder with us, and not to pull up the ladder behind us. Those who have risen to the top owe the greatest responsibility to help the weaker in society. A 'compassionate meritocracy' can help us build a resilient and inclusive society. A 'selfish meritocracy' will divide us and ruin our society.

Goh added that the solution was not to hold people back in the interest of equality of outcomes, or to do away with meritocracy altogether. The solution was to interpret meritocracy with compassion and for people to help one another.

In the education system, meritocracy is generally translated into giving priority in school choices or allocating higher levels of educational resources to those who are with merit. The Singapore education system is highly meritocratic and competitive. Students compete for a place in their school of choice based on merit. Schools compete to attract good students. But meritocracy in such a competitive system presents Singapore with a dilemma. On the one hand, if it leaves children behind by favouring only the ones with 'merit', it risks creating social tensions that may break the society apart. Moreover, as a very small country, Singapore has a limited pool of human resources and cannot afford to leave children behind. On the other hand, if policies are designed to achieve equality among children, the students who can 'fly' may be held back and Singapore could be poorer because of this.

Therefore, in the paradox of compassionate meritocracy, Singapore has to leave no child behind without holding back the children in front. This is Singapore's distinctive way of trying to be equitable. It is not Finland's method of equity, for example. Equity in Singapore education seeks to reconcile meritocracy and humanity. For the ones who can go far based on their own merit, the country does not set an artificial glass ceiling for the sake of equity. The country supports them to 'fly' but also educates them to contribute back to the society that has helped to make them successful. Prime Minister Lee Hsien Loong said:[19]

> If you succeed under our system, then you must feel the duty to contribute back because you did not do it alone. Therefore, if that works, we invest in you, you give back, then everyone will benefit from the system and will see it as fair and good.

For those in the middle, there are more pathways to enhance their chances for success. This will meet the needs of most individuals. For those who are left behind in the meritocratic race, the country pays special attention to them to level them up through direct interventions. Such an approach does not promise an equalisation of outcomes, or even pretend to do so. But every child, it is believed, can have access to an education that will provide a good enough foundation for a meaningful adult life. The country reaches out to different types of learners in different ways. This is unequal in absolute terms, but not absolutely unequal in terms. Every child has a chance for a decent future. The country intends to see to it that every child gets that chance and makes good use of it.

For a country so committed to the principle of meritocracy and also to the competition that is associated with the principle, there is paradoxically another side to the system—a humane one—that appears to be its opposite. This humane side is manifested most clearly in the policies aimed at those who are unable to make it through meritocratic competition.

Compassionate Meritocratic Interventions

According to the OECD, equity in education pays off in terms of student achievements. The OECD found that[20]

> the highest performing education systems across OECD countries are those that combine high quality and equity. In such education systems, the vast majority of students can attain high level skills and knowledge that depend on their ability and drive, more than on their socioeconomic background.

In terms of equity, Singapore is only slightly above the OECD average. But its student achievement is far above the OECD average. So, compared to, say, Finland, Singapore does not fit too well as an example of this OECD finding. Yet Singapore, in its own way, takes equity very seriously.

I will not be surprised if many in the world assume that Singapore concentrates only on top students. However, Singapore is as concerned with students at the bottom of achievement rankings as those at the top. Although Singapore ranked highly in PISA in 2009, it was concerned that some students were shown to be lagging behind. Singapore was concerned with the 'long tail to the achievement distribution' in its 2009 PISA results.[21] The 'long tail' here refers to the fifth percentile scores (low scores) and the difference between mean scores and fifth percentile scores. Although Singapore ranked second, fourth and fifth in terms of mean scores in math, science and reading in PISA 2009, respectively, in terms of fifth percentile scores, the country ranked lower at sixth, thirteenth and ninth. What this suggested was that there was a greater variance or gap between the strong and weak students in Singapore, compared with some other high performing systems. This was a great concern for Singapore, even though the mean score was very high. The finding strengthened the resolve in the country to continue reaching out to those on the bottom rungs of student success actively. The performance by the academically weaker

Figure 4.1 PISA 2009 and 2012 Changes in Percentage of Low Performing Students

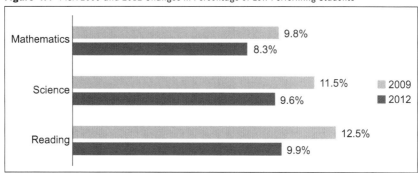

Figure 4.2 PISA 2009 and 2012 Changes in Percentage of High Performing Students

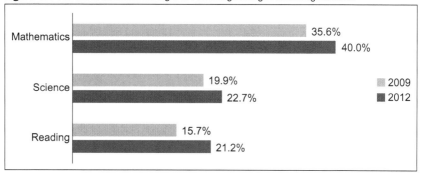

students improved in every domain in the 2012 PISA. Compared to 2009, the percentage of low performers in all domains decreased to less than 10 per cent.[22] The percentage of high performers increased in every domain, too (refer to Figures 4.1 and 4.2).

According to the MOE, these results affirmed the nation's ongoing efforts to support academically weaker students. What are some examples of these efforts? One is the Learning Support Programme (LSP), which was initiated by the MOE in 1992. This programme helps primary one and two students who are weak in English language to catch up. This early intervention programme is crucial because English is used as the language of instruction for other subjects, and many students do not come from English-speaking families. The LSP provides extra lessons in small groups on a daily basis. This learning support has subsequently been extended to mathematics. The Learning Support for Mathematics (LSM) programme, which was piloted in 2001, helps Primary 1 and 2 students who are weak in mathematics to catch up. In 2013, the MOE announced that learning support would be provided for students who have fallen behind in English and mathematics all the way up to the end of their secondary school education.[23]

More recently, there is a greater awareness in Singapore that early childhood education provides an important foundation to schooling and contributes significantly to the holistic development of a child. But low-income families are often unable to afford early childhood education due to financial constraints. Most pre-schools in Singapore are run by the private sector. So, when the MOE began operating its first five state-run kindergartens in 2014, a third of the school places were reserved for children from low-income homes. These kindergartens are located in neighbourhoods that allow them to draw in a good mix of children from low and middle-income families. They are even strategically located near primary schools so that parents can cut down on daily expenses in sending their children to different locations. The Kindergarten Financial Assistance Scheme helps low-income families to send their children to kindergartens. This move is part of how Singapore levels up children from disadvantaged backgrounds.[24]

Singapore has also put in place substantial subsidies for pre-school education, especially for lower income families. In particular, every Singaporean child aged six and below is entitled to a Child Development Account (CDA). The government helps families pay pre-school fees through a top-up to the CDA. The majority of children receive Singapore $600 as a start.[25]

Singapore is also doing more about educating special needs students. Tharman Shanmugaratnam, in his 2015 budget speech, said:[26]

> Our spending on students in our Special Education (SPED) schools has increased over the last five years by 50%. It was already much higher than for students in a regular school, and we have increased it further by 50% in real terms. We have been strengthening the SPED curriculum, helping to train up the teachers. MOE is funding professional development of the teachers in our SPED schools. We are intervening earlier and trying to intervene better.

But what would you do to help children who fail their examinations, even at the primary level, and do not appear to be cut out for a regular secondary school? Under a meritocratic system, they will be left with few choices, other than to struggle in the system, and some will eventually drop out. But in Singapore, the education system reaches out to them in the spirit of compassionate meritocracy. In 2007, the NorthLight School (NLS) was set up to provide an education programme specifically designed to meet the needs of students who failed PSLE one or more times. Given the success of NLS, a second specialised school, the Assumption Pathway School (APS), was set up in 2009. Both NLS and APS were given additional resources and flexibility to help these students find success in their own way. By 2014, another two specialised schools for the Normal (Technical) stream, Crest Secondary School and Spectra Secondary School, were catering to students who were among the bottom 10% of those who passed PSLE. All these specialised schools have received accolades from society for helping their students find identity, meaning and success in life. Indeed, a five-part television series, "Don't Call Us Beaten", was aired in September 2015 to showcase the lives of students and teachers from NLS and APS. Hopefully, the society will come to accept that a failure in examinations is not a failure in life, and will support those who are not so academically inclined to succeed in other ways.

A Case of Compassionate Meritocracy

How does compassionate meritocracy unfold in practice on the ground? Let us take a look at the Assumption Pathway School (APS), as an example of how a school helps students who otherwise would have fallen through the cracks. The APS is one of the two special schools which cater to the group of students who are unable to progress through the mainstream academic school system. Applications by students who have failed the PSLE once are considered based on the recommendations of their primary school principals. Students who have already failed the PSLE twice are given priority in admission over those who failed for the first time. Three hundred students enrolled in 2009, and 700 students enrolled in 2011.

Why may some students, who used to be failing in school, find meaning and success at this school? The APS recognises the profile of their students and designs curriculum and teaching strategies to suit that profile. Courses focus on practical skills. Students learn by doing the work. Their vocational courses, training programmes and curriculum are aligned with the standards set on the Singapore Workforce Skills Qualifications. The school is especially keen to work with industries to provide students with placement for industrial attachments and potential employment when they graduate. The school goes all out to engage partners in different industries such as facilities management, site maintenance, hotels, restaurants and production factories. Learning in authentic workplaces has its own challenges. Teachers accompany their students to the workplaces so that if there are any discipline issues or logistical issues, the teachers are on hand to provide guidance and support.

Even so, the APS encourages its students to have dreams despite their poor past performance. When I visited the school, I was impressed by how the school had created a platform where every student got to choose a challenge for himself or herself for the year. The challenge could be in performing art (for example, doing a musical), a service learning project (for example, going to a third world country to help in an orphanage) or an outdoor adventure (for example, climbing a mountain). Every week, the students met for two and a half hours to prepare for their challenge, which they would undertake at the end of the year. The message was clear: you are entitled to your dream, and you can take action to make your dream come true.

The APS does not just attract students. It attracts passionate and committed teachers, too. (It is one of the few schools in Singapore that can recruit its own teachers.) In fact, when the school started, there were many more applicants than there were teaching positions. Staff members go far beyond their call of duty to help their students. During weekends, some of them hunt for jobs with students who need a job. Others visit absent students in the evening to bring them back to school. Because of the high emotional demands on teachers, the school has to look after the emotional well-being of the teachers too. The staff members rally around one another to share their burdens and generate solutions to student problems.

In Singapore's meritocratic system, the better the results, the better the school the student goes to. But the APS model also suggests that there is paradoxically an 'anti-meritocratic' element in the Singapore system too. The worse the results, the more likely it is that APS will admit the student. The further paradox is that if the APS becomes very successful and provides a good education for academically weak students, parents whose children score borderline passes in the PSLE may be attracted to send their children to the school. But in order to enroll in the well-received programme of the APS, the only way is to do badly enough in the PSLE!

In many ways, Singapore operates classical meritocracy, reaping some benefits and bearing certain consequences. Students who fail are consigned to the 'low status' schools that most people do not wish to choose. In Anglo-American systems, vocational schools are frequently the low status remainder that is left for students who cannot succeed in conventional settings. However, it is not quite like this at the APS. The inspiring mission, the quality of staff and the care that is provided for students as individuals mean that some students and their families actually prefer going to the APS rather than to have the wider choices of future pathways that are in principle available in a more conventionally 'rigorous' setting. Although Singapore is a competitive society, many teachers are drawn to this school to teach, despite knowing how tough it will be.

The APS embodies and illustrates Singapore's paradox of compassionate meritocracy. For a country founded on the principle of strict meritocratic competition so that people with merit are placed on fast tracks to rise to the top, it is paradoxical that there is also a compassionate principle in play to level up those left behind. However, this compassionate meritocratic principle is also not a form of affirmative action for disadvantaged students (for example, to give 'discounts' to them in the examinations) that undermines the principle of meritocracy, academic rigour or the dignity of those who may benefit. Rather, the education system is purposefully reaching out to make sure that 'no child is left behind'. There are alternative pathways for those whose abilities are not in the traditional academic areas. Singapore strives to be meritocratic as well as compassionate, and competitive as well as cohesive. The societal order works, albeit paradoxically, always in tension, requiring great effort and attention to make it work.

Conclusion

Is the American dream possible in Singapore? The answer would have been a clear yes in the past. But would a young Singaporean today, in the same position that his parents were in, be able to see his life chances and those of his children improve in his lifetime? As Singapore matures, this is increasingly difficult. Whether by meritocracy or any other principle, the experiences of other parts of the world suggest that upward mobility tends to decrease in an increasingly matured or less rapidly expanding society or economy. But the question should have been asked another way: Is the Singapore dream still possible in Singapore? Yes, why not? For the Singapore dream is not about an individual striking out for his own success in a land of opportunity. It is about a country that comes together to care for one another, so that no one is left behind or forgotten.

> The Singapore dream is not a dream of simply striking it rich in a land of opportunities.
>
> It is about a country that comes together to care for one another, so that no one is left behind or forgotten.

References

1 Young, M. (1958). *The Rise of the Meritocracy, 1870–2033.* London: Thames & Hudson.

2 Read for example, Bell, D. (1973). *The Coming of Post-Industrial Society.* London: Heinemann.

3 Read for example, Breen, R. & Goldthorpe, J. H. (2001). Class, mobility and merit: The experience of two British birth cohorts. *European Sociological Review*, 17(2), 81–101.

4 Satz, D. (2008). Equality, adequacy, and educational policy. *Education Finance and Policy*, 3(4), 424–443.

5 Arrow, K., Bowles, S., & Durlauf, S. (2000). *Meritocracy and Economic Inequality.* Princeton, NJ: Princeton University Press.

6 Young, M. (1958). *The Rise of the Meritocracy, 1870–2033.* London: Thames & Hudson; Young, M. (2001, June 29). Down with meritocracy. *The Guardian.* Retrieved from http://www.theguardian.com/politics/2001/jun/29/comment

7 Radnor, H., Koshy, V., & Taylor, A. (2007). Gifts, talents and meritocracy. *Journal of Education Policy*, 22(3), 283–299.

8 Lee, K. Y. (2000). *From Third World to First: The Singapore story 1965–2000.* Singapore: Times Publishing; Mauzy, D. K. & Milne, R. S. (2002).

Singapore Politics under the People's Action Party. New York: Routledge; Tan, K. P. (2012). The ideology of pragmatism: Neo-liberal globalisation and political authoritarianism in Singapore. *Journal of Contemporary Asia*, 42(1), 67–92.

9   Barr, M. D. & Skrbiš, Z. (2008). *Constructing Singapore: Elitism, Ethnicity and the Nation-Building Project.* Copenhagen: Nordic Institute of Asian Studies.

10 Cited in Han, F. K., Fernandez, W., & Tan, S. (2015). *Lee Kuan Yew: The Man and His Ideas.* Singapore: Marshall Cavendish.

11 Han, F. K., Zuraidah, I., Chua, M. H., Lim, L., Low, I., Lin, R., & Chan, R. (2011). *Lee Kuan Yew: Hard Truths to Keep Singapore Going.* Singapore: Straits Times Press.

12 Barr, M. D. (2006). Racialised education in Singapore. *Educational Research for Policy and Practice*, 5(1), 15–31.

13 Tan, J. (2008). The marketisation of education in Singapore. In J. Tan & P. T. Ng (Eds.), *Thinking Schools, Learning Nation* (pp. 19–38). Singapore: Prentice Hall.

14 Read for example, Apple, M. W. (2006). *Educating the "Right" Way: Markets, Standards, God, and Inequality* (2nd ed.). New York: Routledge; Ball, S. J. (1993). Education markets, choice and social class: The market as a class strategy in the UK and US. *British Journal of Sociology of Education*, 14(1), 3–19; Gewirtz, S., Ball, S. J., & Bowe, R. (1995). *Markets, Choice and Equity in Education.* Buckingham: Open University Press.

15 Cited in Choo, D. (2012, December 3). PM Lee defends system of meritocracy. *Yahoo! Newsroom.* Retrieved from https://sg.news.yahoo.com/pm-lee-defends-system-of-meritocracy-055639189.html; Ramesh, S. (2012, December 2). Important to Balance Govt's Key Goals for S'pore: PM Lee, Singapore. Retrieved from http://www.channelnewsasia.com/news/singapore/important-to-balance-govt/528002.html

16 Read for example, Nair, P. (2012, December 20). Framing meritocracy as an either-or option unhelpful. *The Straits Times*, p. A30; Davie, S. (2012, November 29). Time to redefine academic success. *The Straits Times*, p. A30.

17 Young, M. (1958). *The Rise of the Meritocracy, 1870–2033.* London: Thames & Hudson.

18 Goh, C. T. (2013, April 29). We need compassion alongside meritocracy. Retrieved from http://news.pap.org.sg/print/news-and-commentaries/commentaries/we-need-compassion-alongside-meritocracy

19 Lee, H. L. (2013, August 18). Prime Minister Lee Hsien Loong's National Day Rally Speech. Retrieved from http://www.pmo.gov.sg/mediacentre/prime-minister-lee-hsien-loongs-national-day-rally-2013-speech-english

20 Organization for Economic Cooperation and Development (OECD) (2012). *Equity and Quality in Education—Supporting Disadvantaged Students and Schools.* Paris: OECD Publishing. (p. 14).

21 Organization for Economic Cooperation and Development (OECD) (2012). *Equity and Quality in Education—Supporting Disadvantages Students and Schools.* Paris: OECD Publishing.

22 Ministry of Education (MOE) (2013, December 3). International OECD Study Shows That Singapore Students Are Ready to Thrive in the 21st Century. MOE Press Release, Singapore. Retrieved from http://www.moe.gov.sg/media/press/2013/12/international-oecd-study-shows-that-singapore-students-are-ready-to-thrive-in-the-21st-century.php

23 Ministry of Education (MOE) (2015, March 6). Infosheet on Levelling up Programmes in Schools. MOE Press Release, Singapore. Retrieved from http://www.moe.gov.sg/media/press/2015/03/levelling-up-programmes-in-schools.php

24 Davie, S. (2013, March 28). Priority plan for places at new MOE kindergartens. *The Straits Times*, p. A1.

25 Tharman, S. (2015, March 5). Budget 2015 Debate Round-Up Speech by Deputy Prime Minister and Minister for Finance, Mr Tharman Shanmugaratnam. Retrieved from http://www.singaporebudget.gov.sg/budget_2015/BudgetDebateRound-UpSpeech.aspx

26 Tharman, S. (2015, March 5). Budget 2015 Debate Round-Up Speech by Deputy Prime Minister and Minister for Finance, Mr Tharman Shanmugaratnam. Retrieved from http://www.singaporebudget.gov.sg/budget_2015/BudgetDebateRound-UpSpeech.aspx

5

PARADOX 3

Centralised Decentralisation

Singapore centralises to achieve synergy.
It decentralises to achieve diversity.

Singapore runs a public school system. Almost all schools in the country are government schools and almost all children go to them. Schools are funded by the government and report to the Ministry of Education (MOE). The MOE develops national level policies and schools implement them with fidelity. It is fair to say from this perspective that Singapore has a centralised education system.

On the other hand, there are different types of schools in the country. There are schools that emphasise art, science, humanities, technologies, sports and vocational education. While they are all funded by the government, each school has different strengths, offers different programmes as well as emphasises different pedagogies to cater to their students. Each school is proud to say in the same breath how it aligns with the national mission and yet develops its own signature programmes that are different from other schools.

The MOE officials will point to the MOE's national imperatives that all schools are implementing. At the same time, they will also talk about school autonomy and about how much power has been decentralised to the schools. So is Singapore a centralised system or a decentralised one? The answer is that Singapore is paradoxically both centralised and decentralised. Centralisation and decentralisation are two sides of the same coin, rather than two ends of a continuum. Singapore's strategy is really one of 'centralised decentralisation'.[1]

How Does Centralised Decentralisation Work?

Firstly, one has to understand that schools in Singapore report to the MOE, not to a school board or local authority. The power to hire or terminate school leaders or teachers resides with the MOE. Schools' accountability is to the government administratively, while the government's accountability is to the citizens democratically. Therefore, in a way, one may regard schools as the local operational units of the MOE. There is a need for a high level of school accountability in Singapore, because the government carries a great responsibility for achieving national educational outcomes and ensuring high value for fiscal spending.[2]

The MOE sets the education policies. Schools carry them out. The accountability system ensures education policies are implemented and education standards are upheld. This fidelity of policy implementation is mentioned quite often in international reports. However, the MOE also encourages innovation and diversity in the schools. So, in implementing policies, schools should understand the policy intention but decide how they would like to carry out the policy. They should not simply follow a top-down approach to education reforms. Instead, in the words of Tharman Shanmugaratnam:[3]

> Quality will be driven by teachers and leaders in schools, with ideas bubbling up through the system rather than being pushed down from the top . . . They are in the best position to develop new approaches to engage their students.

What this approach achieves is 'strategic alignment, tactical empowerment'. A quest for innovation and diversity while maintaining alignment to education policies is the very essence of the paradoxical 'centralised decentralisation' education governance approach of Singapore.[4] With policies as guiding principles, schools are given the space to customise education to the needs of the students and to be innovative in their programmes. The government maintains a certain level of control to ensure that ends are achieved. In the book *The Fourth Way*,

Hargreaves and Shirley argue that governments should steer rather than drive education. Education reform should involve less government and more democracy.[5] However, in Singapore, the paradox is that the government both drives and steers the education system.[6]

In a centralised decentralisation approach, school leaders must develop the skills to wisely adapt the policy initiated by the MOE into their unique school context and deal with all the complexities that may come their way. This is part of the reason why school leaders in Singapore undergo rigorous professional development. With increasing autonomy given to schools, the MOE shifts away from an interventionist role to a supervisory role, albeit in a slow, calibrated way. Schools are encouraged to take ownership of the measures they employ to meet both local and national goals. Such an approach challenges school leaders to think outside the box while doing so well within the box—to find the balance between autonomy and accountability.[7] School leaders find themselves spearheading school-based initiatives while meeting national needs and the standards set within the school accountability system. This is no mean feat. School leaders in Singapore are well accustomed to embracing paradoxes and performing balancing acts.

In essence, the Singapore education system centralises to achieve system level synergy. The system is not merely a loose collection of schools with no central direction. It is a tight knit community of schools coming together to serve the higher order needs of the country, where each school is a crucial piece of the whole. The system decentralises to achieve diversity, innovation and customisation at the school level. It is not a one-size-fit-all system, where all schools are faceless, characterless and merely a piece of the great machinery. The school system aims to be a flexible one, where schools taken together can serve the needs of the different types of learners in Singapore.

Centralised decentralisation can work because of two other related paradoxes that form the foundation for the success of this approach:

- Competitive collaboration
- High accountability, high responsibility

Competitive Collaboration

When visitors come to Singapore to study its education system, they often hear that schools are competing fiercely with one another. But they also learn that schools collaborate and share resources in their school cluster or even nationally. Schools in Singapore are highly competitive and highly collaborative, all at the same time.

A twin paradox to 'centralised decentralisation' in Singapore is competitive collaboration among schools. The philosophy is that of a national team competing in the Olympics. Every player wants to be chosen as a member of the first team. No one wants to be on the substitute bench. So, players should compete with one another to be on the first team. That can lead to improvement. But when a player is chosen, others who have not been chosen should cheer for the chosen player, because when the team wins, everyone wins as a team. That is the spirit of competitive collaboration. This is what schools in Singapore are about—one system for the country.

Such a spirit is not just about joint projects. It is embedded in the basic functioning of the system. When a principal mentors a capable teacher for leadership in a school, the final beneficiary is often another school. When the teacher is ready for a leadership position, the person may be identified by the MOE to be posted to another school that needs this person more or where a better opportunity for further development is available. Many capable heads of department, who have been groomed in one school, become vice-principals in another school. Similarly, many capable vice-principals who have been groomed in a certain school eventually become the principal of another school. So, in Singapore, school leaders know that they are developing people for the system, rather than just for the school. This is a system high in collaboration. School leaders also trust the system to provide the human resources the school needs. This is a system high in trust.

In Singapore, school leaders do not just lead a school. They are called to lead 'nationally'. That means that a school leader belongs to a community of leaders. School leaders care for the whole education system, not just the school each of them is currently leading. They have to take a broader view and consider how their decision in school will affect other schools or even the whole nation. Social capital in Singapore is 'nationalistic'.[8] This is the spirit of competitive collaboration. Centralised decentralisation can work because the spirit of competitive collaboration helps drive improvement while keeping the system united.

High Accountability, High Responsibility

Another important and related paradox in the system that allows centralised decentralisation to work is 'high accountability, high responsibility'. In *The Fourth Way*, Hargreaves and Shirley argue that education should be driven by people who respond to their inner sense of responsibility, rather than the external demands of accountability. In a healthy education system, responsibility should precede and exceed accountability.[9] The paradox in Singapore is that educators embrace and display both responsibility and accountability strongly. In schools, there are strong accountability cultures and structures. School leaders and teachers spend a good deal of their time collecting data, tracking progress and writing reports. But these are merely tasks to be done, not the driving force for improving education. Many educators are in this line of work because of their sense of responsibility towards their students. In Singapore, accountability and responsibility are not two ends of a dichotomy. They are two sides of the same coin.[10]

The main school accountability system in Singapore is the School Excellence Model (SEM). The SEM is a school self-appraisal quality assurance system that helps schools perform systematic self-assessment, identify areas for improvement and benchmark against similar schools.[11] Introduced in 2000 as a replacement for the school inspectorate system, the SEM broadly requires schools to track their own key performance indictors under the categories of 'Enablers' and 'Results'. The 'Enablers' category, which comprises school cultural, process and resource components, is concerned with how schools achieve their outcomes. The 'Results' category, which comprises assessable criteria such as Partnership and Society Results and Key Performance Results, is concerned with the outcomes that the school has achieved. The self-assessment results are validated by an external assessor team once every five years.

Like any other quality assurance system, the assessment process is explicit in requiring evidence to justify a certain score. Moreover, a school should also have evidence of continuous improvement over the years. Therefore, to respond to the stipulations of the SEM, teachers are busy with not just delivering excellent education, but also collecting evidence of that excellence. School leaders cannot merely ensure that their school is doing all the right things. They must also ensure that excellent work is systematically codified, evidence is produced, and trend analysis is done, so as to show that their school is doing better and better. A school leader told me that while he might not exactly enjoy the process of preparing for an external validation, quality assurance was not just for school improvement. Like any other critical services provided by the country, there should be a robust quality assurance system in place so that citizens can trust even more in the public school system.

In my research with school leaders in Singapore, I found that they displayed a strong sense of moral accountability rather than bureaucratic accountability, as they felt that the schools they led were intrinsically linked to the country's future and they had to be good stewards of national resources. Moreover, they were able to embrace a paradoxical mix of both high accountability and high responsibility. They were busy with the operational demands of accountability, but they were driven by their sense of responsibility.[12] In the Singapore teaching fraternity, moral responsibility is harmonious with bureaucratic accountability.

According to many international reports, a major strength of the education system in Singapore is the quality of the teachers. However, the quality of teachers is usually described in terms of qualifications or professional skills and development. There is another important dimension to the quality of Singapore teachers: their inner drive of responsibility. This is a spirit handed down from the pioneer generation of teachers to the present one.

The pioneer generation of teachers exhibited a deep inner drive reflecting their responsibility to engage in nation building, something that was very much needed at a time when Singapore was struggling to build a nation. Their spirit was remarkable, considering that they were themselves young and inexperienced. To quote Heng Swee Kiat:[13]

> Our pioneer educators themselves were young, learning on the job, some-
> times teaching in the afternoon what they had just learnt themselves in

the morning. Some of them were younger than you are now, when they had already started teaching. But our pioneer educators were resourceful and resilient. They rallied together to raise a nation with the limited resources available to them then. In so doing, they laid the foundations for our nation to climb out of poverty towards progress and opportunity, and for our people to step forward with grit and ability.

Singapore celebrated its 50th year as an independent nation in 2015. As part of the year-long celebration, the country honoured more than 700 pioneers during the Pioneer Tribute Dinner, celebrating and paying tributes to the 14,000 strong pioneer educators and staff.[14] The media was helpful in highlighting the work of the pioneers. There was Mrs Mangalesvary Ambiavagar, now 100 years old, former principal of Raffles Girls' Primary, who went the extra mile to make sure children were nourished at a time when nutrition was a key school issue. Mr A. N. Balagopal, now 84 years old, former Commonwealth Secondary principal, who was once posted to remote Christmas Island, had to take three to four days to sail there in choppy waters. Ms Nanda Bandara, now 76 years old, created an eco-pond in Haig Girls' School by sinking a bathtub. The school of course did not have resources for an eco-pond, but the students were interested in science—hence the innovation! These pioneer educators and many more exemplified the inner drive of responsibility. They were trailblazers. The days were hard and the pay was low. The pioneer generation exemplified the values, skills, and dedication needed of every educator in Singapore. They bit the bullet and thrived in a period of great volatility and need. They laid a firm foundation for nation building. Their work was underpinned by the values of resourcefulness, resilience and responsibility. They showed the noblest side of teaching. Singapore is doing its best to continue this pioneering spirit today and into the future. Teachers are encouraged to 'see the big picture' and recognise their part in the Singapore story. Heng Swee Kiat said:[15]

> The next fifty years for us will be similar—there will be a period of volatility, uncertainty, complexity and ambiguity—but probably even more challenging because of the speed of technological changes and the speed of globalisation. In the midst of these challenges, it will be all the more important for teachers to help students develop the values

and strength of character that will form their personal anchors in a world of flux. Our pioneer teachers taught your parents to stand on their own feet and to stand tall. You will do the same, keeping the can-do spirit alive and strong.

Singapore is cognisant that the demand for accountability should not erode the drive of responsibility. In fact, the quality assurance system should support the work of educators, if it is well designed. So, in 2011, when there was growing concern among teachers that the demands of the SEM had somewhat encroached into their time spent on teaching duties, the SEM was simplified and processes were streamlined to reduce the work needed by up to a third.[16]

Singapore's education system currently operates in a complex and dynamic context that is very different from those experienced by the pioneer educators, but the underlying principles are the same. It is said that values have changed as Singapore matured as a society. So, is the inner drive of responsibility still strong in Singapore teachers today? Many teachers told me that had they not been driven by their inner sense of responsibility in teaching their students, they would not have given so much of themselves in the process.

Let us revisit the story of the Assumption Pathway School (APS). Teaching in APS is not just a profession. It is a commitment to a mission to serve those who may otherwise remain at the periphery of society or simply drop out. But it is not easy. Going the extra mile is a mantra for some teachers at the APS. Others live by the principle of 'no one left behind'. The duty of care is clear and indoctrinated in the school. There is a strong belief in the guiding principle of 'connecting lives'. There are a good number of examples of teachers who have gone beyond the call of duty in helping their students. These teachers are passionate about their profession. Work is a labour of love. Many teachers join the school with the ideals of touching lives and making a difference. But the students make a difference in their lives, too, as both sides touch the very fabric of the human soul.

This labour of love is down to earth. It may not be glamourous. It is long-suffering. It does change lives, not in dramatic ways, but quietly and surely. Let me share with you two stories. (I have changed some details to protect the identity of the persons involved.) Student S came from a single-parent family. He was unhappy at home and was not motivated to attend school. He was also having problems with being accepted by his friends. Many mornings, he would leave the house in his uniform and spend the day on buses, travelling from one inter-change to another until he returned home in the afternoon. Teacher T has a heart for the errant students that he handles. In order to disci-pline them effectively, he makes the effort to know them, relate with them and understand the root causes of their misbehaviour. T noticed that student S was very knowledgeable of Singapore's public transport system and started conversing with him on that. He then went on to find out more from the boy about why he did what he did. T managed to convince the boy that he was an ally and that his genuine intention was to help the boy be better and feel happier. T also communicated with the boy's parent to help facilitate clearer communication between the two. With suggestions and guidance from T on how his situation could be improved, S's attendance and behaviour eventually improved over time. S also gained more self-confidence. He finally graduated from APS with an ITE Skills Certificate.

Student U's parents divorced when she was in primary school and her grandmother took care of her. She was often caught in the legal tussle of custody between her father and grandmother, both wanting custody of her but not having adequate financial means to raise her. To make matters worse, both sides were not forthcoming in produc-ing documents for financial assistance, leaving U penniless at times. Understandably, student U was emotionally very fragile and her self-esteem was low. She stayed away from both school and home. Teacher V was an unassuming and caring teacher. He knew about student U's situation, took time to comb her usual hideouts to locate her and ask her to come back to school. He gave U moral support and helped her apply for financial assistance. However, there was an occasion during which U's stepmother took the girl away from school for a couple of months. She accused V of brainwashing the girl and even complained to the MOE. Despite these setbacks, V bravely met with U's parents. It was a tense meeting but his perse-verance paid off. The disgruntled parents finally allowed the student to continue coming to school.

These stories were not uncommon in a Singapore school. This is how responsibility plays out in a school context. It is not required in any accountability system for teachers to walk these extra miles. Wee Tat Chuen, who was the founding principal of APS, and headed the school between 2009 and 2013, shared his experience of leading APS with me. How does such a school achieve both high accountability and high responsibility? According to Tat Chuen, his main leadership strategy was to find the balance between the lifeworld and systemsworld of the school.[17]

The lifeworld of a school is about culture—the essence of values and beliefs, the expression of needs and purposes, and the desires of people. The systemsworld is a world of instrumentalities and of efficient means designed to achieve ends. The former is a world of purposes, norms, growth, and development, and the latter is a world of efficiency, outcomes, and productivity. Both worlds have value and both worlds are important. From Tat Chuen's sharing:[18]

> With proper balancing, the systemsworld and the lifeworld enhance each other. For this relationship to be mutually beneficial, however, the lifeworld must be generative. It must be the force that drives the systemsworld. Either the lifeworld determines what the systemsworld will be like or the systemsworld will determine what the lifeworld will be like. There is a compelling lifeworld in APS.
>
> More than half our students came from lower income families and there were many implications thereof. We had a clear vision of wanting to see every student graduating as a caring person and achieving personal success. We believed that there were many paths to success. Our mission was to ensure our students succeed by helping them to learn, grow and be equipped for their life journey after they graduated from APS. Three principles guided us: Connecting Lives; Nurturing Individualised Growth; Flourishing through Opportunities.
>
> It would be our folly to imagine that a school like APS does not need a strong systemsworld and that a compelling desired lifeworld will see to it that the necessary caregiving and teaching gets done. In fact, it cannot be over-emphasised that we needed a strong systemworld to support a flourishing lifeworld at APS. However, I was always conscious that the lifeworld had to be the generative force and not the other way around.

For APS, the systemsworld of efficiency, outcomes and productivity was concerned with how we identified and reached out to the students in need—those with financial, emotional or learning needs. It was also concerned with how we designed and implemented the learning experiences given that the students had not achieved academic success. It was about how we could identify the right staff to join us, and to develop and engage them in the tasks ahead.

To cultivate a culture of care, the systemsworld needs to ensure a few things are in place: staff has space and time to know the students and their background; a referral system that has clear expectations of who needs to do what at each stage of the helping process; and a structure that brings relevant staff together to dialogue and to ensure that care to each student is adaptive to the needs and circumstances. In all of these processes and structures, school leaders, middle managers and staff members play different roles, each role with a different expectation. Accountability contributes to the strength of this systemsworld. But the lifeworld determines how accountability is administered in the systemsworld. Accountability is based on caring relationships and leadership that is exercised with grace and in truth.

In our beginning years at APS, while we relied on existing processes and structures commonly found in other schools to engage the students, the staff members were actively adapting their approaches to the needs of the students and actively learning from one another. Many teachers found out very quickly that making phone calls to students who were absent could not engage the students and their families effectively. They started visiting the students and their families. If that did not work, they went one step further to seek out the students where these students might be hanging out. Instead of just asking them to return to school at the start, they tried to understand the very deep values and motivations of the students and their families. The teachers also found that initial successes were not likely to be sustainable, and that repeated attempts to engage the at-risk students would have to be expected if they wanted to see real change in the students' lives.

Over the years, I have seen how the level teams have come together to support students of varying needs—the student who ran away from home; the student who had no home to return to because of family issues; and the student with deep emotional wounds because of family tensions.

The system of organised caregiving evolved, as we continuously sought to support the students and nurture the lifeworld we desired at APS.

It has been said that teachers are the most important factor to improving students' learning in schools. At APS, I saw this lived out on a daily basis. The teachers who joined us had applied knowing the challenges they would have to face. We had more than a hundred applying for less than twenty positions when we first started. These staff members brought with them their passion, experience and talents to make a sustained difference in the students' lives. Teachers who advocated students to learn scuba diving and helped them do so; teachers who connected students to baking jobs and then coached them in baking skills after school; teachers who spotted students who were talented in dancing and worked to ensure that these talents were developed further; and teachers who taught students photography skills and then helped them to get paid assignments—these were just some examples of how the teachers sought to make a difference by going out of their way to help the students. These were not prescribed as a teacher's job scope. This was passion. This was responsibility from within.

In the 5 years I have spent at APS, I have observed this again and again: students want to come to a school that cares for them and is able to engage them in authentic learning, challenges and growth. For the school to serve the needs of the students, it needs a strong lifeworld and a strong systemsworld, and for the lifeworld to be the generative force!

Conclusion

On one hand, the Singapore education system is top-down, competitive and accountability-driven. But on the other hand, the system is also bottom-up, collaborative and responsibility-driven. The system is tight at the strategic level and empowering at the tactical level. Like a nice sofa set, its frame is hard, but its seat is soft. Policies point the direction for change. Accountability keeps the system in check. But it is the fraternity of collaborative and responsible educators on the ground that breathes life into the system.

When Singapore first implemented its bilingual policy in the 1960s, not many teachers were trained to teach mathematics, science or other subjects using English. Many teachers were themselves educated in their own mother tongues. Therefore, when they were required to teach mathematics, science or other subjects using English, it was an absolute nightmare for many of them. It was not just a matter of having difficulty learning to teach in English quickly. It was also a psychological barrier to teaching, knowing that one's inadequacy in English was not helpful at all to one's students in learning. But it was a policy that was for the greater good and for the future. Therefore, the pioneer generation of teachers bit the bullet, studied and taught at the same time. It took Singapore many years to reach a stage in which English was finally the language that most teachers could use with confidence in teaching. But in the early years, many teachers who were not English educated gritted their teeth and continued teaching. A generation of young people turned out fine because of the effort of the previous generation.

I remember some of my own teachers who were not English educated but had to teach subjects in English. They struggled with English, and I knew they would have been more effective as a subject teacher if they had taught in their mother tongue. But they persevered. I graduated. That is why as an educator, I often tell my course participants who are school leaders and teachers: Education is the human enterprise of paying it forward. One generation pays the price so that the next generation has a chance in life. Someone paid for us. Now it is our turn to pay it forward. This is the spirit of education in Singapore.

Education is the human enterprise of paying it forward.

References

1 Ng, P. T. (2008). Quality assurance in the Singapore education system: Phases and paradoxes. *Quality Assurance in Education*, 16(2), 112–125; Ng, P. T. (2010). The evolution and nature of school accountability in the Singapore education system. *Educational Assessment, Evaluation and Accountability*, 22(4), 275–292.
2 Ng, P. T. (2010). The evolution and nature of school accountability in the Singapore education system. *Educational Assessment, Evaluation and Accountability*, 22(4), 275–292.
3 Tharman, S. (2005, September 22). *Achieving Quality: Bottom up Initiative, top down Support*. Speech by Mr Tharman Shanmugaratnam, Minister for

Education, at the MOE Work Plan Seminar 2005 at the Ngee Ann Polytechnic Convention Centre, Singapore. Retrieved from http://www.moe.
gov.sg/media/speeches/2005/sp20050922.htm

4 Ng, P. T. (2012). An examination of school leadership in Singapore through
the lens of the Fourth Way. *Educational Research for Policy and Practice*,
11(1), 27–34.

5 Hargreaves, A. & Shirley, D. (2009). *The Fourth Way: The Inspiring Future
for Educational Change*. Thousand Oaks, CA: Corwin.

6 Ng, P. T. (2012). An examination of school leadership in Singapore through
the lens of the Fourth Way. *Educational Research for Policy and Practice*,
11(1), 27–34.

7 Ng, P. T. (2010). The evolution and nature of school accountability in
the Singapore education system. *Educational Assessment, Evaluation and
Accountability*, 22(4), 275–292; Ng, P. T. (2012). An examination of school
leadership in Singapore through the lens of the Fourth Way. *Educational
Research for Policy and Practice*, 11(1), 27 34.

8 Ng, P. T. (2016). Whole systems approach: Professional capital in Singapore. In J. Evers & R. Kneyber (Eds.), *Flip the System: Changing Education
from the Ground Up* (pp. 151–158). New York: Routledge.

9 Hargreaves, A. & Shirley, D. (2009). *The Fourth Way: The Inspiring Future
for Educational Change*. Thousand Oaks, CA: Corwin.

10 Ng, P. T. (2013). An examination of school accountability from the perspectives of school leaders in Singapore. *Educational Research for Policy and
Practice*, 12(2), 121–131.

11 Ng, P. T. (2003). The Singapore school and the school excellence model.
Educational Research for Policy and Practice, 2(1), 27–39.

12 Ng, P. T. (2013). An examination of school accountability from the perspectives of school leaders in Singapore. *Educational Research for Policy and
Practice*, 12(2), 121–131.

13 Heng, S. K. (2014, August 1). Speech by Mr Heng Swee Keat, Minister for Education, at the 2014 Teaching Scholarship Presentation
Ceremony, Grand Copthorne Waterfront Hotel, Singapore. Retrieved
from   http://www.moe.gov.sg/media/speeches/2014/08/01/speech-by-
mr-heng-swee-keat-at-the-2014-teaching-scholarship-presentation-
ceremony.php

14 Heng, S. K. (2014, July 31). Celebrating the Legacy of Education
Pioneers: More Than 700 Pioneers and Guests Experience "Back
to School" Nostalgia at MOE's Pioneer Tribute Celebration, Ministry of Education: Singapore. Retrieved from http://www.moe.gov.sg/
media/press/2014/07/moe-pioneer-tribute-celebration.php;   Schoolbag
(2014, August 4). *Kudos to Our Pioneer Educators!* Schoolbag the Education News Site, Singapore. Retrieved from http://schoolbag.sg/story/
kudos-to-our-pioneer-educators!

15 Heng, S. K. (2014, August 1). Speech by Mr Heng Swee Keat, Minister
for Education, at the 2014 Teaching Scholarship Presentation Ceremony,

Grand Copthorne Waterfront Hotel, Singapore. Retrieved from http://www.moe.gov.sg/media/speeches/2014/08/01/speech-by-mr-heng-swee-keat-at-the-2014-teaching-scholarship-presentation-ceremony.php

16 Heng, S. K. (2011, September 22). Opening Address by Mr Heng Swee Keat, Minister for Education, at the Ministry of Education (MOE) Work Plan Seminar, at Ngee Ann Polytechnic Convention Centre, Singapore. Retrieved from http://www.moe.gov.sg/media/speeches/2011/09/22/work-plan-seminar-2011.php

17 Sergiovanni, T. J. (1999). *The Lifeworld of Leadership: Creating Culture, Community, and Personal Meaning in Our Schools*. New York: Jossey-Bass.

18 Adapted from Wee Tat Chuen's sharing of his thoughts regarding his experiences in leading APS.

6

PARADOX 4

Teach Less, Learn More

> More of the same teaching that did not work previously is not the way
> to inspire better learning.

When cooking a meal and feeding a child, one has to prepare food ingredients and cook them into a palatable dish, before giving the food to the child. To complete the process, the child has to ingest, digest and absorb the food into the body. Teaching and learning is a similar process. The teacher has to prepare the learning ingredients and design a palatable lesson before 'feeding' the child with the material. To complete the process, the child has to ingest, digest and absorb the material in the lesson.

Using the feeding analogy, a common teaching and learning problem is this: the teacher may be very conscientious in wanting to 'feed' the child, but the child refuses to eat! When that happens, what does the teacher do? Teach again! More teaching! More of the same teaching! The teacher shoves the information down the child's throat. If teaching does not succeed at 9 o'clock in the morning, it will be repeated at 4 o'clock in the afternoon. This, in Singapore, is called 'remedial lessons'.

Teachers in Singapore teach a lot. They are very conscientious at teaching, re-teaching and more re-teaching if necessary. But there is an underlying assumption that their students will only learn if they teach. If students do not learn, then the solution is to teach more! But more of the same teaching that did not work is not the way to inspire better learning. To help students learn better, teachers have to understand how their students learn and tailor teaching strategies accordingly. This is analogous to saying that if customers are staying away from a restaurant, the chef may wish to find out what customers like and examine the taste of his dishes. If one keeps serving the same dish that has proven to be unappealing to diners, it is hard to imagine that business will miraculously improve.

When you visit a doctor, one of the things that a doctor must do is to diagnose your problem before giving you medication. Can you imagine a doctor who prescribes two aspirins three times a day regardless of what you are suffering from? The same can be said for teachers. Teachers have to find out why students are not learning instead of just teaching more using the same method. But for some teachers, their teaching methods are fixed regardless of the profile of their students. Their teaching approach has not changed for years! Therefore, the reminder is for teachers to focus less on repetitive teaching as a solution to a learning problem. If teachers teach less but teach better, then students will be able to learn better and be more motivated in their learning. The idea is for teachers to review their teaching with a view to engage their students in the learning process. Learner-centredness is at the heart of pedagogy. This, to me, is the essence of the message of 'Teach Less, Learn More' (TLLM).

What Is TLLM?

TLLM started with Prime Minister Lee Hsien Loong and his National Day Rally speech in 2004. He was explaining that there was a lot that the government had recently done and would continue to do in the education system in terms of provisions and reforms. However, he cautioned that, given more resources, schools should not add more homework or increase the content because that would defeat the whole purpose of the education reform. In fact, he preferred to cut down on some of the syllabi so that there would be less pressure on the children and more space for them to explore. Then he said:[1]

> We have got to teach less to our students so that they will learn more. Grades are important—don't forget to pass your exams—but grades are not the only thing in life and there are other things in life which we want to learn in school.

The phrase 'teach less, learn more' then caught on. Citizens asked about it. The media asked about it. In 2005, the MOE formally launched 'Teach Less, Learn More' (TLLM) as a policy. Tharman Shanmugaratanam, who was then Education Minister, explained that TLLM was a paradigm shift about teaching and learning and was a continuation of TSLN. The objective was to shift the focus of education from quantity to quality. He explained how TLLM could be implemented:[2]

> We will seek to cut back on quantity, careful and calculated cuts, so as to provide more 'white space' in the curriculum, space which gives schools and teachers the room to introduce their own programmes, to inject more quality into teaching, to reflect more, to have more time for preparing lessons and to give students themselves the room to exercise initiative and to shape their own learning.

Just a year before the launch of TLLM, the MOE launched the 'Innovation and Enterprise' (I&E) initiative. I&E aimed to develop intellectual curiosity and a collective enterprising spirit among students.[3] TLLM continued the journey by bringing the I&E spirit into the teaching and learning process. More importantly, TLLM brings into focus the effort at shifting Singapore's performance-driven education based on quantifiable indicators, to quality-driven education based on a broader definition of success and diverse learning pathways. The emergence of the TLLM initiative as part of TSLN is a sign that change in the Singapore education system has shifted from tweaking the macro structures to dealing with the finer aspects of the dynamics of teaching and learning.

TLLM entails a different understanding of knowledge and pedagogy. It is an overarching principle to guide educators as Singapore develops a new learning environment for students, one that emphasises 21st century skills and not just academic content. In the TLLM paradigm, students will be less dependent on rote learning, repetitive tests and standardised instruction. Lessons should engage students through experiential discovery, differentiated teaching, the learning of lifelong skills, and the building of character through innovative and effective teaching approaches and strategies. This 'quality' breakthrough requires teachers to review the 'why', 'what' and 'how' of teaching.[4] It also requires students to become engaged learners: young people who are proactive and interested in the process of teaching and learning. It is envisaged that teachers and students will be involved in a wide variety of learning activities such as brainstorming, problem solving, undertaking real world tasks and even peer teaching using various pedagogical modes such as collaborative learning, problem-based learning and project work.[5]

Large-scale education reforms from other parts of the world have served as valuable lessons for Singapore. From the late 1950s through the 1960s, the United States has launched a series of large-scale national level education reform. There was a suite of initiatives at the system level to reform schools and curriculum. However, after more than a decade, it was clear that other than isolated examples, there was hardly any substantial change in the classroom.[6] Elmore noted that fundamentally, despite the extraordinary costs of making large-scale system level changes, getting teachers to change their practices in their daily work was a far more complex process than what many policy makers had anticipated.[7] With the great pressure and incentives to undertake innovations, many schools adopted high-sounding reforms but only implemented them superficially. On paper, there were changes. In reality, the dynamics of teaching and learning in the classroom were untouched.

Singapore understands this. Singapore recognises that education reform is not just about tweaking macro structures. The effort must reach the fabric of schools and alter the nature of instruction and interactions in the classrooms. Altering system level structures alone does not necessarily translate into achieving engaged learning among learners.[8] I often say to school leaders and teachers in Singapore that students do not experience policies. They experience their teachers. That is why beyond the system level structures that were put in place, TLLM attempted to reach into the very fabric of schooling—the dynamics of teaching and learning in the classroom. This of course is easier said than done.

There are three aspects of engaged learning: affective, behavioural and cognitive. Students who are affectively engaged find learning interesting, rewarding and motivating. Students who are behaviourally engaged see the relevance of learning in school to their lives. Students who are cognitively engaged find intrinsic motivation in undertaking challenging learning tasks which require substantial intellectual effort.[9] To help teachers understand and implement TLLM, the principles for engaged learning were disseminated in a 'Toolkit for Engaged Learning and Teaching' to all schools in 2005. According to the toolkit, students are engaged when teachers[10]

- select pedagogy that is suitable for their students' learning styles;
- design a learning experience that stretches thinking, promotes interconnectedness and develops independent learning;
- create a classroom environment that is safe, stimulating and engenders trust;
- adopt assessment practices that provide timely feedback regarding student performance and information to improve learning; and
- select relevant, authentic and meaningful learning content for students.

Determining whether education has moved from 'quantity' to 'quality' is tricky. Some of the 'signposts' are as follows:[11]

- Construction of knowledge, not just transmission of knowledge
- Understanding of content, not just memory of facts
- Mindful pedagogy, not just mindless activities
- Social constructivism, not just individual study
- Self-directed learning, not just teacher-directed tasks
- Formative assessment and self-assessment, not just summative grades
- Learning about learning itself, not just learning about a topic

Each of these signposts represents an important shift in the nature of teaching and learning in the Singapore education system.

Another difficult issue regarding the implementation of TLLM in Singapore is to reconcile it with the learning of content and examination performance. Does TLLM imply that learning content is no longer important or practice is redundant? Does TLLM imply a sacrifice of examination results? Not quite. Singapore is currently developing high technology industries, such as life sciences and biomedical engineering. This requires graduates with solid grounding in the relevant knowledge domains. The learning of content remains important! However, the current curriculum is quite crammed with content. Thus, some trimming of content is warranted. But trimming of content does not mean that students learn only skimpy outlines!

Practice is also not redundant. There is a saying that 'repetitive practice' stifles creativity. But some learning really requires frequent practice. Have you ever heard of a concert pianist who does not practice regularly? Try driving in the heart of London or New York after you have not driven for ten years and see what happens. So, TLLM does not belittle the value of practice. It is important to practice what you learn. But it is not helpful to 'over-practice' examination questions, to the detriment of a holistic learning experience.

Consider the analogy of learning Chinese martial arts. If you learn Chinese martial arts from a master, he may make you do a lot of exercises to strengthen your body before teaching you the strokes. You may not feel really excited about those repetitive exercises, but he makes you do them anyway. If you are only interested in the fanciful strokes, when it comes to a contest, your opponent will not be defeated by your snake or crane strokes. He will collapse laughing. Your strokes are fanciful but not impactful! TLLM is not form without substance. TLLM is about students learning more and better, not less and worse! So, if TLLM is really about better pedagogy and engagement, and students are learning what they ought to be learning, there is no reason why results should drop. In fact, barring an implementation dip, results should improve in the long run!

Even so, what are students expected to learn more of? Consider this example. Two chess grandmasters compete in the finals of the chess competition. Both have studied all the opening moves. Both have studied all the end games. Both have many years of experience. In a way, both have acquired all the conventional knowledge about chess. So who wins? The one who is least trapped by conventional knowledge and can make the unexpected and devastating move wins! Therefore, there are two parts to the challenge of TLLM. Students have to learn the conventional knowledge solidly. Then they have to learn not to be trapped by the conventional knowledge so that they may be adaptable and innovative. Students need to learn more of the skills that make them adaptable to a new world that this generation has not experienced, but into which they will grow for their life and work.

So there ought to be a good balance of content and thinking skills in TLLM. Teachers must have the pedagogical ability to engage students in the enjoyable aspect of learning while helping them acquire the important content of the subject and the relevant thinking skills. Teachers should not misinterpret TLLM to mean simply fun activities for students. The focus is still on learning. The potential pitfall is that while there are new activities, at a deeper level, students are still acquiring knowledge through traditional learning methods and teachers are still teaching with traditional pedagogies. The teaching-learning dynamic is unchanged, but now disguised using new activities. In a classroom, activities without pedagogy are, well, just activities without pedagogy. Activities are good, provided they are well thought through to bring about learning.

Has Singapore reached its TLLM destination? Hardly! A journey from quantity to quality is a long, continuous one. Personal habits in teaching and learning die hard! Culture takes a long time to change. The outcome so far has been mixed. Student engagement and teacher professionalism have improved, but the pressure cooker environment due to high stakes examinations and parents' expectations remains.[12] However, Singapore is keeping at it faithfully and celebrating every little success. This journey is an aspiration, not a destination.

After more than a decade of TLLM, the phrase may have faded into the background. Teachers' attention is focused on newer initiatives to be implemented. But the underlying philosophy of shifting the focus from quantity to quality has not changed. So, as the education system evolves, it will continuously calibrate itself to try to achieve the best of both worlds: depth and breadth, knowledge and skills, teacher-taught and student-led learning, individual results and collective learning. Balance is imperative but the focus should be on the central thesis of 'less is more'.[13]

To change something as personal as one's teaching style or learning habit is challenging to say the least. Teachers and students will have to come to terms with their new identity brought about by the epistemological paradigm shift. In the new paradigm, teachers of engaged learning are designers of learning opportunities. They are no longer mere providers of information and solutions. They have to create a learning environment where students work meaningfully and collaboratively to solve problems and do authentic tasks. They facilitate learning through guidance and mentoring. In a world where students can easily search for information on the internet, teachers need to be willing to go along with their students in a journey of knowledge discovery.

In the new paradigm, students ultimately have to take ownership of their learning journey. They have to learn to plan for themselves and be independent in their learning. Certainly, a considerable degree of maturity is needed from both the students and their teachers. Students have to feel secure about not being spoon-fed. Teachers have to feel secure about letting go of their control of the entire teaching and learning process. This, as some teachers told me, is a very difficult hurdle for a Singapore teacher to cross. Teachers with many years of teaching experience in traditional pedagogy will also have to be open to experimenting with new pedagogical approaches. They have to keep abreast of the changes in the education landscape. Singapore has many platforms for teacher development, including coaching, mentoring and Professional Learning Communities (PLCs). They are very useful learning platforms. But, within these platforms, a greater effort is necessary among teachers and school leaders to challenge their own presuppositions about teaching and learning. Without critical reflection and a will to change, mentoring and sharing of practices may perpetuate outdated approaches rather than champion new ones. Thus there are two aspects of the TLLM change process: sharing of rich experiences in the field brings a system up to a certain extent. Challenging existing mindsets brings about the breakthrough. Singapore is still stronger in the former than the latter. It needs to work harder on challenging people's mindsets.

Can TLLM develop children's creativity? From my perspective, children already are creative. When they are young, they are curious. They ask a lot of questions, some which adults actually have no answers to. They are imaginative. Look at them play! Playing is highly creative. They act out what they see in movies, often in groups, and everyone wants to be the hero. They are the dramatists. They can express themselves—until they go to school. Then they lose it. They become disinterested. They become inhibited. Therefore, the challenge is to allow children's natural creativity to flourish in school through engaged learning in meaningful learning tasks in a whole-some learning environment. Children have creativity. Schools should nurture it, not kill it. This is a critical part of the TLLM challenge.

ICT in Education

Another area of education that is closely linked to the efforts of TLLM is the use of information-communication technology (ICT) in teach-ing and learning. Singapore's current ICT Masterplan 4 represents a great opportunity to take TLLM further. Having implemented ICT Masterplans 1, 2 and 3 from 1997 to 2014, Singapore has established the infrastructure necessary for teaching and learning using ICT. The whole country is highly wired. The technological penetration rate is high. Wireless internet connectivity is found in every school com-pound. Most schools have their own Learning Management Systems (LMS). A majority of teachers and students have their own laptops or other mobile devices. The challenge is now for teachers and students to use ICT powerfully in the teaching and learning processes. Technol-ogy has the power to help teachers design curriculum that can achieve personalisation, choice, challenge, enjoyment, breadth and depth. E-discussion forums allow many students to participate in a discussion at the same time—something that cannot be achieved in a conven-tional classroom. ICT expands access to education and allows students to access learning materials anytime and anywhere, unconstrained by physical time and space. The MOE is currently developing an online Student Learning Space (SLS) to provide all students in the country (regardless of school) access to quality digital learning resources.

However, the focus of Singapore's efforts is not on ICT per se. Rather, the main aim is to encourage and empower teachers to discover how ICT can enable more learner-centred and engaging curriculum and pedagogies. Teaching and learning is a highly contextual process. ICT is a means of enhancing this process. It is not an end in itself. Teachers should not be using technological tools for the sake of using them, even if the tools are elaborate. Many schools are now experi-menting with modular approaches, flipped classrooms and e-learning. Singapore is mindful that it is important to build the capacity among teachers for this kind of change.

ICT will become increasingly important in education, in terms of both quantity and quality of usage. Will teachers become redundant? Hardly! Paradoxically, with the rising presence of technological devices, the human teacher will be more important than ever before. In an era of social media and chat rooms, teachers have to educate students in the ethical use of technology. Teachers also have to develop the students' ability to deal with a large volume of information on the internet, and to discern misinformation from good information. This involves, on the part of the teacher, a high level of expertise in synthesizing information and facilitating student learning. Classroom teaching time will become more valuable because it will be reserved for higher order thinking, rather than didactic teaching. When virtual learning spaces become increasingly used in learning, having a physical learning space and having direct interaction with a human teacher may one day come with a premium! No matter how hard Singapore tries to promote ICT in education, it is never at the expense of the importance of skillful, committed and caring teachers.

However, there is a potential blind spot. In the fabric of the teaching and learning process, students are predominantly treated as kids in a system run by adults. This does not mean that student voice is absent in Singapore schools. In many Singapore schools, students run their own student bodies and play leadership roles in their co-curricular activities. They can give feedback to their school through various platforms. Each year, some 500 or more students from various pre-university institutions come together at the Pre-University Seminar to discuss national level issues from their perspectives. However, in the teaching and learning of content subject areas, teachers are still fully in charge. This is a sub-optimisation of human intelligence.[14]

Twenty-first century learners are digital natives. Some, if not many, students are more savvy with technology than their teachers. Therefore, it is imperative to recognise students as important contributors in the collective intelligence of the entire school system.[15] These digital natives are tremendous sources of progressive approaches to learning. They have been exposed from the youngest ages to a great deal of digital know-how, literally at the tip of their fingers. They use various modes of virtual connectivity on a daily basis that influence their ways of learning and communication. Students should be brought more powerfully into the co-construction of the social and technological context where teaching and learning takes place. Instead of teachers asking themselves how they could use technology for their students, teachers should ask their students how technology could be wrapped around students to help them in their learning! This is an area that Singapore needs to work harder on.

Where is Singapore heading in the area of technology in education? In 2015, the National Research Foundation (NRF) of the Prime Minister's Office launched a Science of Learning Initiative, which aims to develop a scientific understanding of the effectiveness of Singapore's education methods and to develop new methods to achieve better learning outcomes.[16] The initiative hopes to develop cognitive theories and neuroscience-informed technological interventions to enhance learning.[17] Brain-based research is envisaged to lead to innovation in ICT-enhanced pedagogy. Another important area is cyber wellness. The government sets up an Inter-Ministry Cyber Wellness Steering Committee (ICSC) to spearhead efforts to support cyber wellness education. Currently, intensive research is conducted to examine how positive use of the Internet and mobile technologies among young people can be encouraged and supported. Areas that are examined include cyber security and protection against cyber-crime; healthy cyber-gaming; cyber-addiction and cyber bullying; and even parenting roles, knowledge and skills for cyber wellness education for their children. These are still in early stages of development, but it is clear that Singapore has embarked on a timely and increasingly urgent change.

Encouraging TLLM

But how does a country encourage curricular and pedagogical change among schools? In very practical ways indeed! The MOE supported TLLM by introducing the 'TLLM Ignite!' package in 2008 to provide funding for school initiatives in curriculum customisation, differentiated instruction, as well as inquiry-based and problem-based learning. Since 2008, this package has helped spread interesting ideas in teaching and learning which were worth exploring. By 2009, more than half of the schools in Singapore have shared their school-based curriculum innovations in various publications and platforms locally. Some schools have even shared their TLLM initiatives at international conferences.[18]

According to the MOE, an evaluation of the TLLM efforts across the system suggested that teachers had increased their ability to customise curriculum, as well as use a variety of pedagogies and assessment modes. By the end of 2010, some three-quarters of the schools in Singapore have tapped into resources and expertise offered by the MOE in their school-based innovations. According to some teachers, TLLM has encouraged them to be more innovative in their pedagogy, and time dedicated to lesson planning has also increased.[19] Since the launch of the TLLM in 2005, a variety of programmes and school initiatives have sprouted island-wide in response to it.

Here are a few examples to give you an idea of the changes that took place in schools after the introduction of TLLM.[20] At Tampines Primary School, pupils learned about social studies through drama, or story-writing through comic strips. These interesting lessons made learning a thoroughly engaging affair. These lessons were the result of the school's Practices of Effective Teaching and Engaged Learning (PoETEL) framework, launched in 2006. PoETEL is a framework for lesson planning and execution, lesson evaluation and professional development. A school-based curriculum innovation under the TLLM auspices, PoETEL has helped teachers take a more holistic view of teaching, considering five domains of Learning Outcomes, Content, Process, Intellectual Climate and Social Emotional Climate. PoETEL has brought about many positive changes in the school's lessons. Pupils became more engaged and enjoyed their lessons more. Lessons became livelier and more collaborative in nature.[21]

At Fuhua Primary School, pupils who were milling about in small groups around the classroom froze all of a sudden at the sound of a drumbeat. As part of a choreographed move, one group of pupils then responded to a teacher's command by swiftly enacting a scene from a story before freezing once again. The teacher gave another command and a different group of pupils delivered another part of the drama. In another class, pupils learn to give feedback to each other's presentation. All these were part of a drama programme launched in 2011. This programme originated as part of a TLLM Ignite! Project and was an integral part of the English Language curriculum designed to expose pupils to new vocabulary and cultivate their ability to listen, understand and express themselves.[22]

At Jurong Secondary School, part of the Secondary 1 science curriculum was redesigned in 2007 based on the Problem-Based Learning (PBL) pedagogy. Students were presented with real life problems to investigate and solve. In one case, a resident wrote a letter to the press expressing concern about the impact of human activities on the ecosystem in Jurong Lake Park. Using this as the problem, the students worked in groups to investigate the issue and present their findings and solutions. According to feedback from some students, the PBL approach was interesting, meaningful and made it easier for students to learn science. Beyond scientific knowledge, students picked up skills such as teamwork, research, presentation and independent learning. Some teachers also felt that this was an opportunity to learn new pedagogies and try them out in the classroom.[23]

An important point about these examples is how schools are willing to share what they have done in a system that coordinates sharing efforts to facilitate innovation diffusion. The current challenge is to examine whether some of these innovations can be harnessed for system-wide scaling up. But while Singapore can encourage experimentation and innovation in schools by very practical means of coordination, support and funding, educational change is also in the mindsets of people. Teachers in Singapore have grown accustomed to helping students achieve test scores for many years. Will their mindsets change? This is a crucial question. After more than a decade of TLLM, what do teachers now understand to be 'quality education'? I asked this question of middle leaders in school, because they were the teachers who led other teachers and taught in classrooms themselves.

According to my research findings, 'quality education' to them is one that emphasises holistic development, equips students with the knowledge and skills for the future, inculcates students with the right values and imbues students with a positive learning attitude.[24] For example, one of them articulated that

quality education is an education that develops a child holistically. For example, besides doing well academically, values must also be taught. In addition, soft skills like planning and making decision for their own future should be imparted along the way. Also interpersonal skills and team working skills must be imparted to prepare them for the future.

Another said that quality education is one that

> best prepares the students for life; to meet the future challenges of being able to find their identity in a vocation that best fit their abilities and interest; being able to contribute to society; raising a family; and enjoying the fulfilment of personal and professional goals . . . The challenge today is to continue to reshape education so that our students are equipped with the skills and knowledge to help them become independent learners who can adapt and thrive easily in any environment.

Quality education can be achieved if it is delivered by quality teachers, is enabled by sound teaching and learning processes, and occurs within a conducive learning environment.[25] As one participant elucidated succinctly, "Quality education is quality teaching, quality learning and quality relationship between teacher and student." The participants gave some examples of quality teaching, including the use of

- different pedagogies for different abilities students;
- guidance and feedback on how students can improve;
- high order thinking questions; and
- concept maps for students to help them see interconnectedness.

Regarding quality learning on the part of students, a few examples mentioned by the participants were

- students are motivated to learn through active participation in class;
- students demonstrate the willingness to find out how to improve their learning; and
- students ask different types of questions to clarify and to probe assumptions.

Interestingly, the research participants placed emphasis on both academic achievement and learning enjoyment.[26] One participant explained how there should be "a right balance between academic and non-academic achievement" and that the students ought to put in the "effort needed to attain results", but "they are not stressed by the everyday demands to achieve excellence but are given opportunities and platforms to learn a variety of subjects and skills".

The most interesting finding of the entire research project was that the participants did not refer to any measurable indicators (such as PISA results) when they thought about quality education. Instead, they referred to the softer and nobler aspects of education.[27] But if quality education is about committed teachers, superior pedagogy, positive learning attitudes and high order thinking skills, this might also explain Singapore's sterling results in international tests!

Is Singapore Mathematics TLLM?

In early 2015, the internet was abuzz with a mathematics problem many deemed too complex for the average primary or secondary school student. This particular mathematics word problem essentially asked students to determine the exact birthdate of a fictitious girl named Cheryl. This problem, which was mistaken as a 'regular' question that the average Singapore 11-year-old student was supposed to solve, was hailed as an example of the rigour of mathematics taught in Singapore. (I understood that it was actually a question from the 2015 Singapore and Asian Schools Mathematics Olympiad contest paper for secondary school students.) A former mathematics teacher in an independent school in the UK was reported to have commented that "an average student in the UK would panic if presented with this problem and would not even attempt it because pure logic-based questions are not part of the curriculum".[28] Search the internet and you can easily find similar reports elsewhere in the world. 'Singapore mathematics' is an international enigma.

A solid numeracy skills foundation has a tremendous impact on an individual's success, both in school and afterwards.[29] It may arguably be the main aspect of current education reforms in the West, particularly the US and the UK, which look to Singapore's mathematics programme as a model for their own systems.[30] Many countries are buying Singapore textbooks and claiming that they are more effective. According to the OECD, Singapore students possess high levels of motivation, engagement and confidence in learning, particularly in mathematics. Singapore students are highly motivated to learn mathematics and are confident about performing a range of mathematical tasks.[31] Singapore outperforms the US and other participating countries from Europe in international standardised assessments. But what is it specifically about the Singapore mathematics approach that differentiates it from those of other schools systems? Is there something special about Singapore mathematics?

Let us first hear what overseas users of Singapore mathematics have to say about it. A research project in 2010 revealed a significant improvement in student performance in Massachusetts when they adopted Singapore mathematics in their state curriculum.[32] In particular, Garfield Elementary School in Revere, Massachusetts, was reported as having demonstrated improvements in their student performance since implementing Singapore mathematics:[33]

> Three years ago, Garfield started using Singapore Math, a curriculum modeled on that country's official program and now used in about 300 school systems in the U.S. Many school systems and parents regard Singapore Math as an antidote for "reform math" programs that arose from the math council's earlier recommendations. According to preliminary results, the percentage of Garfield students failing the math portion of the fourth-grade state achievement test last year fell to 7 percent from 23 percent in 2005. Those rated advanced or proficient rose to 43 percent from 40 percent.

According to a mathematics teacher from New Jersey in another study:[34]

> Singapore mathematics lessons begin by engaging students in hands-on learning experiences followed by pictorial representations, which help them form a mental image of mathematical concepts. This is followed by an abstract stage, where they solve problems using numbers and symbols. This approach makes the learning of mathematics fun and meaningful, and helps students develop positive attitudes about math.

An impact study in the UK, released in February 2015, further asserted that Singapore's approach to teaching and learning mathematics indeed improved numeracy skills of primary and secondary students.[35] According to researchers at the Centre for Longitudinal Studies, the Singapore approach to teaching mathematics reduced the need to repeatedly revisit material and promoted depth of understanding over memorised procedures.[36]

So, what is the secret? Actually, there is no secret and there is no magic. In fact, I think many mathematics teachers in Singapore will grin if you ask them the secret of 'Singapore mathematics'. The way Singapore teaches mathematics is just trying to follow a basic understanding of good pedagogy, without being too dogmatic to follow a particular school of thought. Mathematics in Singapore generally builds upon the developmental theory that children need to understand concrete examples first before they can fully grasp abstract concepts. Students understand mathematical concepts better by moving from concrete to abstract.

Whenever possible and appropriate, Singapore mathematics teachers ask students to go through some activities that help them connect mathematics with real life (which is especially helpful during the foundation years). Students draw pictorial representations as a step from something concrete towards something abstract (again when appropriate). One of the techniques that Singapore is now famous for is the 'bar model' method (a pictorial method taught to primary school students to solve arithmetic word problems). This is merely a technique, a visual strategy (pictorial representation) to solving word problems. For more advanced learners (say in secondary school), it is sometimes difficult to connect everything in mathematics to real life or use pictorial representation, but this is not necessary. The more important idea is to connect their current topic with their prior learning so that mathematics makes sense to them.

In terms of teaching, the explanation and the presentation of heuristics must be clear. There must be logical scaffolds to help students develop mathematical concepts and skills systemically. The mastery of conceptual understanding and heuristics go hand in hand. However, Singapore teachers do try to practice some instructional differentiation based on learner profiles. For students who are less mathematically inclined, there is an effort to trim the material in terms of cognitive demands and instead focus on more hands-on learning tasks in the classroom. Students then practice a variety of questions so that they can really apply their knowledge. If they cannot apply their knowledge in different situations, they have not fully grasped the concepts yet. Practice is important because they need to be technically competent, so that any higher order thinking can be accompanied by the technical competence to execute the complete problem solving process.

The last point about practice is important. To be a world class table tennis player, one would need many hours of practice to achieve a very high level of competence. That competence gives the player the time and space, within a split second, to consider what to do when receiving a smash from an opponent and execute a return that can turn defence into attack! World class players always look as though they have time to think, although the entire movement takes place within a split second! How can they move so quickly yet still have the time to think? That is because they are so competent that their mental space is freed up for creativity, not execution! Consider the Masterchef competition. Even if the competitors have an appreciation of what fine cuisine should be and have a wonderful idea for their dish, if they cannot produce the dish within the time given, they are out! They must be so competent that they have time and space for creativity!

So in mathematics, when children have to solve a word problem, the problem solving part is to abstract the information and formulate a set of equations to be solved. The solving of the set of equations is the technical part. Children should have technical competence to solve the equations because they have had sufficient practice (but not over-practice). If children do not even have technical skills to solve a set of equations, their mental space will be overcrowded in figuring out both problem solving and equation solving. In fact, problem solving can be practiced up to a certain extent. Once children are familiar with solving certain types of questions, they are psychologically attuned to solving problems that are somewhat similar. The part that Singapore hopes to achieve as a quantum leap is to get children to be able to solve problems that are not familiar, and to be unafraid of them.

But one area of strength in Singapore's mathematics education is this: Singapore does try to prepare mathematics teachers to hit the ground running the moment they start teaching in school after initial teacher training. They are prepared to be able to teach across a range of mathematics topics. They are not just taught general principles, given one or two examples, and expected to apply these principles at school without further guidance. They learn the pedagogies associated with a range of topics and practice them before becoming a qualified teacher. They are further mentored in school after becoming a beginning teacher. The philosophy is a continuous cycle of learning and practicing.

Thus mathematics success in Singapore is not magic. It is pedagogy. Singapore is still trying to improve. Like many areas of learning, form and substance are equally important. Hard work and practice free up thinking space for creativity. The challenge now is to make sure that the creative space is more fully and profitably utilised.

Conclusion

Singapore recognises that education reform has to be deep enough to change the nature of instruction and interactions in the classrooms. TLLM is not just a message for Singapore teachers but one for many others in the world. If teachers teach less but teach better, students will learn more and learn better. The challenge, which will continue for many years to come, is for teachers to improve the teaching and learning processes, and for students to become fully engaged in learning.

Children have creativity. Nurture it; don't kill it.

References

1 Lee, H. L. (2004, August 22). *Our Future of Opportunity and Promise.* Prime Minister Lee Hsien Loong's National Day Rally 2004 Speech at the University Cultural Centre, NUS. Speeches and Press Releases. National Archives of Singapore, Singapore. Retrieved from http://www.nas.gov.sg/archivesonline/speeches/record-details/77f762e5-115d-11e3-83d5-0050568939ad

2 Tharman, S. (2005, March 9). Parliamentary Reply by Mr Tharman Shanmugaratnam, Minister for Education, at the Singapore Parliament. Retrieved from http://www.moe.gov.sg/media/parliamentary-replies/2005/pq09032005.htm

3 Ng, P. T. (2005). Innovation and enterprise in Singapore schools. *Educational Research for Policy and Practice*, 3(3), 183–198.

4 Tharman, S. (2005, September 22). *Achieving Quality: Bottom Up Initiative, top down Support.* Speech by Mr Tharman Shanmugaratnam, Minister for Education, at the MOE Work Plan Seminar 2005 at the Ngee Ann Polytechnic Convention Centre, Singapore. Retrieved from http://www.moe.gov.sg/media/speeches/2005/sp20050922.htm

5 Tharman, S. (2005, September 22). *Achieving Quality: Bottom Up Initiative, top down Support.* Speech by Mr Tharman Shanmugaratnam, Minister for Education, at the MOE Work Plan Seminar 2005 at the Ngee Ann Polytechnic Convention Centre, Singapore. Retrieved from http://www.moe.gov.sg/media/speeches/2005/sp20050922.htm

6 Goodlad, J. I. & Klein, M. F. (1970). *Behind the Classroom Door*. Worthington, OH: Charles A. Jones; Sarason, S. (1971). *The Culture of the School and the Problem of Change*. Boston: Allyn & Bacon; Gross, N., Giacquinta, J., & Bernstein, M. (1979). *Implementing Organizational Innovations*. Berkeley, CA: McCutchan; Fullan, M. & Pomfret, A. (1997). Research on curriculum and instruction implementation. *Review of Educational Research*, 47(1), 335–397.

7 Elmore, R. (1995). Getting to scale with good education practices. *Harvard Educational Review*, 66(1), 1–26.

8 Ng, P. T. (2008). Educational reform in Singapore: From quantity to quality. *Educational Research for Policy and Practice*, 7(1), 5–15.

9 Ministry of Education (MOE) (2013). *Engaging Our Learners: Teach Less, Learn More*. Singapore: Ministry of Education.

10 Ministry of Education (MOE) (2013). *Engaging Our Learners: Teach Less, Learn More*. Singapore: Ministry of Education.

11 Ng, P. T. (2008). Educational reform in Singapore: From quantity to quality. *Educational Research for Policy and Practice*, 7(1), 5–15.

12 Today (2012, August 24). Teach less, learn more—Have we achieved it? *Today*, p. 4.

13 Ng, P. T. (2008). Educational reform in Singapore: From quantity to quality. *Educational Research for Policy and Practice*, 7(1), 5–15.

14 Ng, P. T. (2010). Educational technology management approach: The case of Singapore's ICT Masterplan Three. *Human Systems Management*, 29(3), 177–187.

15 Ng, P. T. (2010). Educational technology management approach: The case of Singapore's ICT Masterplan Three. *Human Systems Management*, 29(3), 177–187.

16 National Research Foundation (NRF) (2015, June 4). Science of Learning Initiative Call for Proposals for Planning Grants. NRF, Prime Minister's Office, Singapore. Retrieved from http://www.nrf.gov.sg/funding-grants/science-of-learning#sthash.CCQS9jMg.dpuf

17 National Research Foundation (NRF) (2015, June 5). National Research Foundation Science of Learning Initiative Planning Grant Guidelines for Participants. NRF, Prime Minister's Office, Singapore. Retrieved from http://www.nrf.gov.sg/docs/default-source/default-document-library/20150605_nrf-sol-planning-grants-application-guidelines.pdf?sfvrsn=0

18 Ministry of Education (MOE). (2010, April 26). Teach Less Learn More. Parliamentary Replies. MOE, Singapore. Retrieved from http://www.moe.gov.sg/media/parliamentary-replies/2010/04/teach-less-learn-more.php

19 Ministry of Education (MOE). (2010, April 26). Teach Less Learn More. Parliamentary Replies. MOE, Singapore. Retrieved from http://www.moe.gov.sg/media/parliamentary-replies/2010/04/teach-less-learn-more.php

20 You can read more examples at https://www.schoolbag.sg/features/teaching-learning

21 You can read more at https://www.schoolbag.sg/story/holistic-teaching-through-poetel#.V2YX7z9f2po

22 You can read more at https://www.schoolbag.sg/story/learning-through-action-and-drama#.V2YYTz9f2po

23 You can read more at https://www.schoolbag.sg/story/problem-solving-in-jurong-lake-park#.V2YYsz9f2po

24 Ng, P. T. (2015). What is quality education? How can it be achieved? The perspectives of school middle leaders in Singapore. *Educational Assessment, Evaluation and Accountability*, 27(4), 307–322.

25 Ng, P. T. (2015). What is quality education? How can it be achieved? The perspectives of school middle leaders in Singapore. *Educational Assessment, Evaluation and Accountability*, 27(4), 307–322.

26 Ng, P. T. (2015). What is quality education? How can it be achieved? The perspectives of school middle leaders in Singapore. *Educational Assessment, Evaluation and Accountability*, 27(4), 307–322.

27 Ng, P. T. (2015). What is quality education? How can it be achieved? The perspectives of school middle leaders in Singapore. *Educational Assessment, Evaluation and Accountability*, 27(4), 307–322.

28 Espinoza, J. (2015, April 14). When is Cheryl's birthday? The tricky maths problem that has everyone stumped. *The Telegraph*. Retrieved from http://www.telegraph.co.uk/education/educationnews/11534378/When-is-Cheryls-birthday-The-tricky-math-problem-that-has-everyone-stumped.html

29 Organization for Economic Cooperation and Development (OECD) (2013). *PISA 2012 Results in Focus—What 15 Year Olds Know and What They Can Do with Qhat They Know*. Paris: PISA, OECD Publishing.

30 Garner, R. (2015, June 18). Singapore-style teaching helps solve problem of maths failure, says new research. *The Independent*. Retrieved from http://www.independent.co.uk/news/education/education-news/singaporestyle-teaching-helps-solve-problem-of-maths-failure-says-new-research-10327085.html; Jackson, B. (2012, October 10). My view: America's students can benefit from Singapore math. *CNN Schools of Thought*. Retrieved from http://schoolsofthought.blogs.cnn.com/2012/10/10/my-view-americas-students-can-benefit-from-singapore-math/

31 Organization for Economic Cooperation and Development (OECD) (2013). *PISA 2012 Results in Focus—What 15 Year Olds Know and What They Can Do with What They Know*. Paris: PISA, OECD Publishing.

32 Wang-Iverson, P., Myers, P., & Lim, E. W. K. (2010). Beyond Singapore Math's textbooks—Focused and flexible support for teaching and learning. *American Educator*, Winter, 28–38.

33 Hechinger, J. (2006, September 12). New report urges return to basics in teaching math. *The Wall Street Journal Online*. Retrieved from http://www.wsj.com/articles/SB115802278519360136

34 Jackson, B. (2012, October 10). My view: America's students can benefit from Singapore math. *CNN Schools of Thought*. Retrieved from http://schoolsofthought.blogs.cnn.com/2012/10/10/my-view-americas-students-can-benefit-from-singapore-math/

35 Jerrim, J. & Vignoles, A. (2015, February). *Mathematics Mastery Overarching Summary Report*. London: Institute of Education, University of London.

36 Center for Longitudinal Studies (2015, June 18). East Asian Teaching Method Leads to "Small But Welcome Improvement" in English Pupils' Maths Skills. Center for Longitudinal Studies, Institute of Education, London. Retrieved from http://www.cls.ioe.ac.uk/news.aspx?itemid=428 7&itemTitle=East+Asian+teaching+method+leads+to+%E2%80%98small +but+welcome+improvement%E2%80%99+in+English+pupils%E2%80% 99+maths+skills&sitesectionid=27&sitesectiontitle=News

III

THE FOUR DREAMS

7

DREAM 1
Every School, a Good School

When I asked someone in the United States what he thought about a vision of 'Every School, a Good School', his reaction was "You must be joking!" He asked me whether the Singapore minister or the US secretary said it. He asked me whether 'No Child Left Behind' has been replaced with 'No School Left Behind'. The United States was still reeling from the latest campus shooting. 'Every School, a Good School' was unfathomable. He observed grimly that at the rate his district was going, it would soon be 'No Good School Left'. If I were to tell someone in Singapore that "Every school is a good school", the person would probably say, dismissively, "Every school is a good school, but some schools are just *better* than others!"

In a way, 'Every School, a Good School' is not a new idea. Deputy Prime Minister Teo Chee Hean, who was then Education Minister, said in 1999:[1] "We have no failing schools in Singapore; only good schools, and very good schools". However, the context and motivation at that time was different. The minister was trying to explain that:

> We often think of the best schools and universities in Britain and the United States and compare ourselves unfavourably against them. The truth is our top schools are not far behind and even comparable to top schools abroad. What is more important is that our average schools are far better than average schools in most countries. High quality education is not reserved for the brightest or richest pupils; it is delivered to all.

Now, due to the publicly available TIMSS, PIRLS and PISA results, Singaporeans in general do not have a problem with accepting that the average Singapore school is better than the average school in most countries. The problem is that most Singapore parents do not want their child to be studying in an *average* school. Most parents, if possible, want their child to be in an *elite* school! But what 'Every School, a Good School' is trying to articulate is that every school offers a good education. There is no need to get into elite schools in order to receive a good education and find success in life. Instead of being fixated on getting their children into these schools, parents should find a school that is suitable for their children. So, how should one understand what a good school is? According to Minister Heng Swee Keat:[2]

> A 'good school' is one that nurtures engaged learners; enables teachers to be caring educators; and fosters supportive partnerships with parents and the community. Indeed it is possible. And each of our schools is good in its own way—as long as we continue to take into account the unique needs and abilities of our students.

But if you ask any school leader in Singapore, he or she will tell you that all schools in Singapore are already trying very hard to be the good school that the minister has indicated. So, the main challenge is not getting the schools to be good schools. The main challenge is to redefine what a good school is in the minds of Singaporeans, including educators, parents and the society at large. Good schools are not just those at the top of ranking tables. A good education does not mean producing the best score in an examination. In a good school, teachers develop their students holistically, not just academically. In a society where every school is a good school, parents focus on their children's overall development instead of just their grades. In the job market, employers hire and promote workers based more on abilities and skills than paper qualifications.

To a certain extent, all schools in Singapore are indeed good schools. The MOE goes to great lengths to ensure that all schools are safe environments for children and young people. Classrooms are generally orderly environments, conducive to the learning that is taking place. Violence is rare. Drugs are non-existent. (Singapore has very severe penalties for drug offences.) The high standards in public education mean that children do get a decent education, regardless of the school their parents decide to send them to. The question is the extent in which parents embrace and act according to this belief. 'Every School, a Good School' is an exhortation to the society to trust in the entire system, not just the highly ranked schools. Every school will strive for excellence in its own way to provide a good education to the students it serves. One does not need to go to an elite school to receive a good education.

But Some Schools Are Just Better than Others, Right?

A vision is a vision precisely because the current picture is not quite what the vision paints. In the media, there are many debates as to whether every school is indeed a good school and that the school that one comes from does not really matter. In a meritocratic society, where academic performance has been seen for a long time as the most viable means to improve social mobility and generally one's lot in life, it is not easy for Singaporeans to embrace the philosophy of 'Every School, a Good School'. Most people will still want their children to go to an elite school, if they can. Others are skeptical of how good a neighbourhood school (a euphemism for non-elite school) can be. Whether it is true or otherwise, the perception is that when comparing an elite school with a neighbourhood school, there is a significant difference in the quality of education, or just the company their child will keep.

So, even if every school is a good school, some schools are just better than others, right? The desire to get into one of those better schools is so intense among parents that they are willing to become volunteers at the schools just to be placed on a higher priority list for the Primary 1 Registration Exercise. In Singapore, this exercise is a high anxiety event for every Singaporean parent with a six-year-old child. This exercise is run over seven phases. At each phase, a certain category of children is given the priority to register. For example, Phase 1 registers a child who has a sibling studying in the primary school of choice. For some popular schools, all the vacancies are filled way before the final phase is reached. At a certain phase, if the number of applicants exceeds the number of vacancies, a balloting exercise is conducted at the school. This balloting exercise can be a heart-stopper for some parents. Imagine anxious parents in a school hall where some scream when their child hits the jackpot, while others sigh with disappointment when the last name is announced. Details of the registration successes, vacancies and balloting results are updated on the MOE website to assist parents throughout the process.[3]

The intense competition for Primary 1 registration among parents stems from the uncertainties each year in securing a place for their child in their school of choice. Therefore parents try to make sure that the child qualifies for an earlier phase of registration. The fourth phase (called Phase 2B) gives priority to children of volunteers of the school (who have contributed at least 40 hours of voluntary service to the school and have been a volunteer for at least a year), active community leaders, or members of a church or ethnic clan directly connected with the school. Of course, this is meant to encourage and recognise parent volunteerism. But this practice of giving priority to children of school volunteers now becomes a means of securing priority school registration. Some parents sacrifice time volunteering at their child's prospective school to earn 'credit', so that their child will have a better chance of enrolling in the preferred school. According to reports in the news, some parents have put in up to 80 hours of volunteer work. Others have tried to use clan or church connections. But despite their efforts, parents applying to certain popular primary schools still have to go through a ballot to secure a place for their child because these schools had many more applications than vacancies. One parent, who had put in about 40 hours of volunteer work with his wife, declared that he would not continue to volunteer at the school anymore when he learned that placement was not guaranteed.[4] To cope with the surge of parent volunteers, one popular primary school raised the requirement to 80 hours and another limited the number of parents who were allowed to be volunteers. In 2014, five popular primary schools decided to scrap their parent volunteerism scheme mainly because the number of people wanting to become parent volunteers greatly outnumbered the volunteer opportunities in the school.[5]

The situation is similar in the secondary school sector. Parents also aim to get their children into the 'better' schools there. In 2015, after a sterling performance by that year's PSLE cohort, the minimum entry requirement of popular secondary schools was also raised.[6] Thus it is a moving target—getting into these schools is a matter of winning the competition among prospective students, and better PSLE results do not guarantee a place. One category of popular schools is the ones offering the Integrated Programme (IP). A local journalist wrote:[7]

> To date, I have had 17 e-mail messages and calls from parents asking me to help them gauge their children's chances of getting into a secondary school of their choice. Of the 17, only two asked me about a non-Integrated Programme school . . . So the hankering after IP schools has still not abated, despite the Government's urgings. The Government needs to examine why parents are not buying the argument that there are many paths to success and every school is a good school. I took the opportunity to ask the parents eyeing IP schools, such as Raffles Institution and Raffles Girls' Secondary, why they were not convinced. One of them had done an analysis of the Overseas Merit Scholarships given out by the Public Service Commission. Not surprisingly, the overwhelming majority of those receiving the scholarships came from the IP schools.

The chairman of the Public Service Commission (PSC) (the authority that appoints and promotes senior public servants, upholds the conduct and discipline of the Public Service, and awards PSC scholarships), noting the perennial general perception that scholarships were only granted to students from top junior colleges, clarified that the PSC would guard against elitism and that potential scholars were carefully assessed. The PSC increasingly looked for character traits and leadership potential in its scholars, not just excellent grades. The PSC would like public service officers to come from diverse socio-economic backgrounds in order to avoid any 'groupthink'.[8] Indeed, things have already begun to change. In 2011 and 2012, only 60% of students granted scholarships were from top schools such as Raffles Institution and Hwa Chong Institution—a drop from 82% in 2007. Students from many other schools have also emerged as scholarship awardees.[9] In 2015, one of the PSC scholarships went to a national table tennis player to pursue Liberal Arts at the Yale-NUS College. She had graduated from Republic Polytechnic with a Diploma in Sports and Leisure Management. Another scholarship went to a student, who was a strong advocate of community service and volunteered regularly at a hospice, to read social work at the University of Auckland.[10]

Yet, research conducted by National University of Singapore (NUS) researchers showed that the loss of a top-50-ranked school (due to its relocation) caused prices in the private housing market to decline by

8.5% for the 1 km school zone and 12.2% for the 1 km to 2 km school zones. The comparable declines in public housing prices were 5.1% and 2.4%.[11] Parents are so fixated on 'good' schools that even property prices are significantly affected by school location. Access to good schools is clearly an emotive issue in society. During a panel discussion at the Asia Education Expo in 2013, a vice-principal of a neighbourhood school reportedly raised the following question:[12]

> How many of our leaders and top officers who say that every school is a good school put their children in ordinary schools near their home? [Only] until they actually do so are parents going to buy [it].

'Every School, a Good School' of course raises the classic chicken and egg, which-comes-first conundrum. On the one hand, bottom schools will not have a chance to become better if the parents are not willing to 'take a chance' on these schools. On the other hand, parents will ask why they should be the first to take that chance when the system of gaining priority access to further education through examination results is still in place. Prime Minister Lee Hsien Loong acknowledged these realities and conceded that change would not happen overnight:[13]

> We have an excellent education system. But our society is getting more stratified. Competition is intensifying amongst our students and the focus, unfortunately I think, is too much on examination performance and not enough on learning. It is very hard to fight these forces because parents want the best for their children and they think the examination results are what make the difference. But I think we need to recalibrate to keep our system open and to focus on things which matter more than exam grades in the long run. But the education system is a very complicated and delicate machinery. You can say what you like or do not like about it; you cannot just push it and expect it to become better. You must find the right spot, fine tune, make the precise adjustment and then watch carefully to see whether it has become better.

Promoting 'Every School, a Good School'

So, how does a country try to promote 'Every School, a Good School'? Here are a few examples of the concrete steps that the MOE has taken. In 2012, the MOE announced the abolition of the banding of schools according to their academic performance.[14] This league table system, which started in 1992, was long regarded by the public as a sort of sacred cow in the education system, although absolute ranking was replaced by broader banding in 2004. The abolition of banding was a bold and strategic move by the MOE to change the mindset of Singaporean parents and the general public that schools should be categorised according to their academic results in national examinations.

With the ministry's thrust for a more student-centric and values-driven education, the excellence and recognition framework for quality assurance in schools was re-aligned to support this. Initially, the Masterplan of Awards (MoA) scheme, established in 2000, was proposed to promote improvements in school performance and recognise school excellence. But in 2012, the MOE decided to revise the schemes into a simpler framework, to be implemented in 2014. This meant that there would be less administrative work for schools and would debunk the perception that schools were encouraged to chase awards instead of focusing on holistic education. The MoA was replaced with recognition for schools with best practices in five areas—namely, Teaching and Learning, Student All-Round Development, Staff Development and Well-Being, Character and Citizenship Education, and Partnership.[15] The MOE also decided in 2012 to cease publishing the names of top scorers in all national examinations. This was another indicator of its proactive approach to redressing over-emphasis on academic results and shifting the emphasis towards valuing students' holistic development.[16] The reaction of society was mixed. Some felt it was the right signal. Others were skeptical that this could serve its purpose. Some even wondered what the problem was with celebrating success and reading about students who had done well.

Several other measures have been implemented in order to send the message that every school is a good school. In 2012, the MOE announced that it would allocate S$55 million over the next 5 years to encourage schools to build on their areas of strength that would distinguish them from others. The areas established by schools included Design Thinking, Outdoor Education, Applied Learning and Aesthetics.[17] By 2013, about 73% of secondary schools and 66% of primary schools have already established a distinctive area of strength.[18]

To further support every school as a good school, the MOE is now encouraging and supporting every secondary school to develop an Applied Learning Programme (ALP) and a Learning for Life Programme (LLP) by 2017. The vision is for all secondary schools to have distinctive programmes that help students apply knowledge and develop life skills. For each programme, every secondary school will receive S$50,000 per year from the MOE. That is a total of S$100,000 per year of extra funding to ensure that all secondary schools are well-resourced to provide holistic education for their students. Moreover, for schools with more students on financial assistance, the amount of Opportunity Fund, a government grant used to provide co-curricular development opportunities for Singaporean students from lower income families, will be proportionately increased.[19] Today, many primary and secondary schools have developed an ALP and an LLP. The aim is to allow all students (not just those who can win awards) to have opportunities to engage in learning activities beyond the classroom and beyond pen and paper.

Principals are also systematically appointed to and rotated through various schools across the entire system.[20] This strategic distribution of principals allows seasoned principals to share best practices with a new school that may be struggling in its performance. It also gives seasoned principals opportunities for professional development as they take on new and uncertain challenges in their new school. Indeed, in 2013, the MOE decided to deploy some of the nation's most experienced and well regarded principals to take on the leadership of neighbourhood schools. These principals bring to the schools their vast knowledge, experience and best practices in school leadership and change.[21] It is a signal to parents that the MOE pays attention to all schools, not just the popular ones, and that it is determined to make sure that every school is indeed a good school in Singapore. This appears to have had an effect on some parents. One newspaper reported that a parent had placed her son in a brand new school despite advice from people not to take risks with her son's future in a school without a track record. This parent had apparently looked to the school leaders, who had previously led 'popular' schools, for assurance that her children would be in good hands.[22]

The media has been helpful in highlighting good work done by all types of schools, not just the 'elite' ones. For example, the main newspapers have carried reports of Crest Secondary School, the first school for students in the Normal (Technical) stream, where most of the children performed poorly in mathematics and other foundation level subjects at the PSLE. According to Crest's teachers, the vocational modules helped illustrate the relevance of schooling to the students. The school is equipped with classrooms that are designed like an actual supermarket store or a store selling handy tools, to provide students with more realistic learning environments for the vocational modules. Crest has gotten off to a promising start with its students. Although about half of its students come from disadvantaged families, attendance has been high at 97%.[23]

Other neighbourhood schools have been given the limelight as well. Choa Chu Kang Primary School has been integrating subjects such as science, mathematics, and arts with robotics since 2008. Using robotics to teach these subjects made learning enjoyable for the students. Furthermore, students could exercise their creativity in designing robots. The school's principal observed that this programme developed students' information gathering and critical thinking skills. Indeed, in 2008, the school received an MOE award for their Programme for School-Based Excellence in Robotics.[24] Other neighbourhood schools have also risen to the occasion in the examinations. Some have demonstrated examination performances comparable to their more illustrious counterparts. Jing Shan Primary School, for example, was highlighted in the media for making commendable progress in recent years to the point that their overall pass rate for 2013 was 98.4%, which was above the national average of 97.5%.[25] These examples, highlighted in the media, send the message to the society that elite schools are not the only ones that can provide quality education for their students.

Recently, instead of recognising schools for producing high examination results, Singapore schools have also been recognised for their efforts and achievements in providing their students with holistic education. For example, in 2015, CHIJ St. Joseph's Convent, Clementi Town Secondary School and Serangoon Garden Secondary School received the Lee Hsien Loong Award for Innovations in the Normal Course. These schools had developed innovative practices that led to significant benefits in the all-round development of their students in the Normal (Academic) and Normal (Technical) Courses.[26]

'Every School, a Good School' is fundamentally about a change in mindset about schools in the society. In my interaction with school leaders, many expressed the sentiment that all schools were good in their different ways. Every school caters to the specific needs of its students. Every school would like to work with parents to develop their children. However, it remains hard to convince society not to be so competitive about enrolling in 'elite' schools. The challenges to addressing this issue include the ingrained public perception of certain schools, the aspirations of some parents who live their dreams vicariously through their children and the desires of school alumni to maintain the prestige and image of their schools.

In many ways, the education system is a reflection of societal values and expectations. The education system could potentially continue with the current societal norms of competing for schools and focusing narrowly on grades and examinations, but instead, Singapore has decided to act with boldness and resolve to embark on a major transformation of mindsets and influence societal values and expectations.

Conclusion

Recently, a few parents and students have bucked the trend of opting for elite schools when they could. For example, a student who was awarded the president's scholarship in 2013 chose to enroll in the Singapore Sports School rather than any of the elite schools that he could have gotten into.[27] Occasional examples do not necessarily imply a change in societal attitudes, but the initial signs are encouraging. This vision is compelling. Regardless of whether Singapore can one day arrive at a stage when citizens all agree that every school is a good school, the important thing now is for the vision to drive the education system and indeed the society in the desirable direction.

'Every School, a Good School' is part of Singapore's way of equity. It does not provide absolute equality. But it does mean that the baseline standard is high enough so that any advantage that comes from family background is no longer a significant factor in one's future success. If indeed every school is a good school, then every child will have a chance in life, regardless of his or her background. There should be no need to compete to get into an elite school.

'Every School, a Good School' is also part of Singapore's way of soul searching about what is important in life. If Singaporeans are overly competitive, good will never be good enough. Heng Swee Keat argued:[28]

> Education alone cannot give us a good life, and we need to be clear what a good life is. If a good life is simply about getting ahead of others, and achieving the 5Cs (Cash, Condominium, Cars, Credit Card, and Country Club), the competitive pressure in the workplace will define how we as parents and teachers view education. Then no amount of changes in the education system can alter the reality of each of us chasing after material and positional goods. We cannot have broader definitions of success in education without our society accepting broader definitions of success in life. In many respects, the education system reflects societal norms and expectations.

In a system where schools compete to attract better students, 'Every School, a Good School' is also a reminder to educators that every school serves a part of the society. Every school is an important school. If it educates the high performing students, it is an important school—it develops many future leaders for the country. If it educates the low performing students, it is an important school—it gives hope to kids who otherwise may not have had a chance in life. Every school is a good school. Every school is an important school. This is a part of how compassionate meritocracy plays out in practice. It is the spirit of education in Singapore.

References

1 Teo, C. H. (1999, July 16). Speech by Radm (NS) Teo Chee Hean, Minister for Education and Second Minister for Defence, at the Chinese High Lecture at the Chinese High School. Retrieved from http://www.moe.gov. sg/media/speeches/1999/sp160799.htm

2 Heng, S. K. (2012, September 12). Keynote Address by Mr Heng Swee Keat, Minister for Education at the Ministry of Education Work Plan Seminar at Ngee Ann Polytechnic Convention Centre. Retrieved from http://www.moe.gov.sg/media/speeches/2012/09/12/keynote-address-by-mr-heng-swee-keat-at-wps-2012.php

3 Ministry of Education (MOE) (2014, May 15). Registration Phases and Procedures. Retrieved from http://www.moe.gov.sg/education/admissions/primary-one-registration/phases/

4 Teng, A. & Lee, P. (2013, July 23). No guarantees for parent volunteers at popular schools. *The Straits Times*, p. B6.

5 Lee, P. (2014, June 10). Primary 1 registration: 5 things to know about the popular parent volunteer scheme. *The Straits Times*, p. B2; Lee, P. (2014, June 10). Schools closing door on parent volunteer scheme. *The Straits Times*, p. B2.

6 Teng, A. (2015, December 24). Cut-off points up for popular secondary schools. *The Straits Times*, p. A6.

7 Davie, S. (2012, November 29). Time to redefine academic success. *The Straits Times*, p. A30.

8 Heng, J. (2013, September 18). PSC reaches out to students from diverse backgrounds. *The Straits Times*, p. B2.

9 Chan, R. & Heng, J. (2013, September 18). PSC seeks more diversity in scholarships. *The Straits Times*, p. A1.

10 Lee, R. M. (2015, July 22). Hospice volunteer, table-tennis player among 75 new Public Service scholars. *Today*, p. 4.

11 Sumit, A. & Sing, T. F. (2015, December 17). How school proximity affects house prices. *The Straits Times*, p. A26.

12 Ang, Y. (2013, November 21). "Soft skills just as vital as exams", say educators at Asia Education Expo. *The Straits Times*, p. B2; Chiu, P. (2013, November 21). Jurong West Secondary Vice-Principal Takes Issue with "Every School Is a Good School" Ideal: Yahoo Newsroom, Singapore. Retrieved from https://sg.news.yahoo.com/jurong-west-secondary-vice-principal-takes-issue-with-%E2%80%98every-school-is-a-good-school—ideal-103224519.html

13 Lee, H. L. (2013, August 9). Prime Minister Lee Hsien Loong's National Day Rally 2013. Singapore: Prime Minister's Office. Retrieved from http://www.pmo.gov.sg/mediacentre/prime-minister-lee-hsien-loongs-national-day-rally-2013-speech-english

14 Ministry of Education (MOE) (2012, September 12). MOE Removes Secondary School Banding and Revamps School Awards. Press Release. Retrieved from http://www.moe.gov.sg/media/press/2012/09/moe-removes-secondary-school-b.php

15 Ministry of Education (MOE) (2012, September 12). MOE Removes Secondary School Banding and Revamps School Awards. Press Release. Retrieved from http://www.moe.gov.sg/media/press/2012/09/moe-removes-secondary-school-b.php

16 Davie, S. (2013, November 23). Shifting focus on scores to learning. *The Straits Times*, p. A6.

17 Heng, S. K. (2012, September 12). Keynote Address by Mr Heng Swee Keat, Minister for Education at the Ministry of Education Work Plan Seminar at Ngee Ann Polytechnic Convention Centre. Retrieved from http://www.moe.gov.sg/media/speeches/2012/09/12/keynote-address-by-mr-heng-swee-keat-at-wps-2012.php

18 Ministry of Education (MOE) (2013, April 2). Making Every School a Good School. Parliamentary Replies. Retrieved from http://www.moe.gov.

sg/media/parliamentary-replies/2013/08/making-every-school-a-good-school.php

19 Ministry of Education (MOE) (2014b, July 9). Every School a Good School. Parliamentary Replies. Retrieved from http://www.moe.gov.sg/media/parliamentary-replies/2014/07/every-school-a-good-school.php

20 Ministry of Education (MOE) (2013, October 11). Ministry of Education Appoints 60 Principals in 2013. Press Release. Retrieved from http://www.moe.gov.sg/media/press/2013/10/ministry-of-education-appoints-60-principals-in-2013.php

21 Heng, S. K. (2013, October 10). Speech by Mr Heng Swee Keat, Minister for Education, at the National Institute of Education (NIE) Leaders in Education Programme Graduation Dinner, the Regent Singapore Hotel, Singapore.

22 Tan, A. (2015, July 27). New kid on block, but leaders with track record. *The Straits Times*, p. B10.

23 Chia, S. (2013, April 30). A taste of success at Crest Secondary School. *The Straits Times*, p. B4.

24 Chia, S. (2012, June 19). Robots spur pupils to solve problems creatively. *The Straits Times*, p. B4.

25 Lai, L. (2013, November 23). Faith in heartland school pays off. *The Straits Times*, p. A6.

26 Ministry of Education (MOE) (2015, September 21). Recognising Best Practices in Holistic Education. Press Release. Retrieved from http://www.moe.gov.sg/media/press/2015/09/recognising-best-practices-in-holistic-education.php

27 Teng, A. (2013, November 26). Choosing schools that best fit them. *The Straits Times*, p. B2.

28 Heng, S. K. (2013, October 10). Speech by Mr Heng Swee Keat, Minister for Education, at the National Institute of Education (NIE) Leaders in Education Programme Graduation Dinner, the Regent Singapore Hotel, Singapore.

8

DREAM 2
Every Student, an Engaged Learner

In the 1990s, I taught mathematics to students who were 17 and 18 years old. These were very bright students, placed generally at the top band of their cohort in national examinations. One day, as I was teaching the topic of differentiation, I asked my students, "What do you get when you differentiate a function?" My students responded, "We get the answer!" In fact, my students were rather incredulous that their teacher would ask such a question. But the response reflected a very pragmatic dimension in the learning psyche of a typical Singaporean student. He or she may be very good at getting the right answer but may not appreciate or even care about the rationale behind the answers.

Engaged learners are the foundation of the Learning Nation that Singapore aspires to be. To make learning a national culture, students must become engaged learners from a young age. According to Minister Heng Swee Keat,[1]

> Every Student an Engaged Learner is based on our core belief that every child can learn—not just in school, but for the rest of his life. As educators, we want to nurture engaged learners who are motivated, enjoy learning, and go on to fulfill their potential.

So, a significant change in the education system is to develop the engaged learner. Basically, the engaged learner that is referred to here is someone who has an intrinsic motivation for learning and has an attitude of lifelong learning. This is what education should be like in Singapore, as Prime Minister Lee Hsien Loong said:[2]

Education is not just about training for jobs. It is about opening doors for our children, and giving them hope and opportunities. It is more than filling a vessel with knowledge—it is to light a fire in our young people. They are our future.

So, the current vision for schools is for every student to be an engaged learner, whose attention, energy and intellect are completely focused upon the object of learning in the lessons. An engaged learner is also one who is able to self-regulate learning; plan the learning process strategically; collaborate with others to enrich their learning experience; and find excitement, pleasure, or fulfilment in the learning process.[3] An engaged learner is an outcome of TLLM. What are some of the issues and challenges that Singapore schools face in developing and nurturing engaged learners?

Being a Student in Singapore Can Be Tough!

On one hand, many Singapore students are diligent learners. They put in long hours at school and with homework. They prepare well for tests and examinations. On the other hand, many lack the enthusiasm of a curious learner. They seldom express interest in delving deeper into an area of learning beyond what is stated in the syllabus. There are a few reasons why.

Stress from Examinations

Most students are very focused on examinations and grades. They are often under pressure from parents, teachers or themselves to excel in the examinations and obtain good grades. At this moment, examination results still determine to a large extent the future academic pathways—which schools one can apply to. Even during the holidays, a considerable number of students registering for PSLE or 'O' Levels that year opt to spend time studying instead of taking the time to rest and recharge for the next semester. A parent wrote to the press:[4]

> One 16-year-old from the Express stream sitting her 'O' levels this year had to go back to school for five hours of lessons daily for a fortnight during the school holidays. That is almost a regular school day. And she

had 20 practice examination papers to complete. That's 120 hours of classes and homework over four weeks, or 30 hours per week. In other words, about three-quarters the load of an adult working full time.

Trying to attain academic achievements is one of the most commonly reported sources of stress for adolescents, as they spend considerable amounts of time in school.[5] A dialogue session between MOE and randomly selected students, conducted in July 2013, surfaced various concerns of students over the pressures of taking the PSLE. One student said that the "teachers put too much importance on it, over-emphasising it, over-pressurising the students. They give such a scary picture of what would happen next if we don't do well".[6] Indeed, the examination pressure associated with high stakes examinations often robs students of the joys of learning. They are consumed, for that crucial period of time, by the preparations needed for them to ace a test that will heavily influence their opportunities for academic advancement. Moreover, there is a societal culture that perhaps over-values academic results to a point that there is a stigma about not performing well.[7] Some students observed that "the PSLE creates a social hierarchy and will cause those who score better to look down on those who don't do well". Another student felt it was impera-tive that they obtain a good result in their PSLE because a poor one "leads to discrimination; people feel lousy when they are put in certain streams".[8]

In 2015, the Singapore Examinations and Assessment Board (SEAB) decided to publish full PSLE papers from previous years to "allow parents to have a clearer picture of the overall expectation of the PSLE".[9] SEAB's decision to do this was to provide students with a practice platform so that they could have a sense of the time they would be given to do a whole set of questions, thereby lessening their anxiety when sitting for the exams. However, the moment the papers were released, parents snatched copies off the shelves of local bookshops. Some purchased multiple copies to keep one at home and send others to school with their child.[10] The pressure had not diminished. The problem is not with the practice of publishing full examination papers. It is with the mindset of people. The problem is in the culture.

Stress from School Work and Homework

In 2013, a Singapore newspaper reported:[11]

> The June holidays began last Saturday. But some children, as well as their parents, are doubtful that they will have much time to enjoy the mid-year vacation. Last Saturday, Prime Minister Lee Hsien Loong posted a photograph of a water theme park on his Facebook and Instagram websites. Accompanying the photograph was the caption: "Today is the start of the June holidays. Happy holidays to all students. Enjoy yourselves, and don't do too much homework!" Mr Lee's Facebook post has since amassed almost 9,000 likes. However, students—as well as their family members—commented that they are bogged down with homework during the month-long holidays.

In a way, it was quite incredible that the prime minister had to remind students to enjoy themselves and not do too much homework during the holidays! But besides the pressure they feel about performing well in the national examinations, students in Singapore also have to deal with academic stress on a daily basis,[12] including during the holidays!

According to the OECD, in a comparison among students of similar socio-economic backgrounds who attend schools which have similar levels of resources, those who attend schools where students devote more time to doing homework perform better in mathematics than those who attend schools whose students devote less.[13] Thus homework is an important factor in learning outcomes. In Singapore, homework is traditionally an important part of the learning process of any child. In 2014, the OECD ranked Singapore third in the average number of hours per week spent on homework at 9.4 hours, just behind Shanghai-China (13.8 hours) and Russia (9.7 hours). In contrast, students in Finland reported that they spend less than three hours per week doing homework.[14]

When these figures were published in the news, there was a high level of public interest. Students, when interviewed by the media, claimed that they spent even more hours than those indicated in the report. One Secondary 3 student reckoned that she spent about 10 to 15 hours per week on homework alone, excluding time for private tuition and extra-curricular activities.[15] Another Secondary 3 student shared that in order to avoid feeling overwhelmed by the amount of homework she needed to complete, she stayed in school to work on it together with her peers. This encouraged her and her friends to discuss questions together and motivate one another to finish homework faster.[16] Parents also observed that there was homework given in every school subject. They claimed that the volume of homework was often a result of teachers failing to coordinate with one another in terms of the amount of assignments children were expected to accomplish on a school night.[17] Yet many teachers also told me that some parents would get upset if their children were not given enough homework. Thus they dished out lots of homework, so that parents would not complain that the teachers were not responsible enough.

Of course, one of the main reasons for the long hours spent on homework is the examinations-oriented mindset in Singapore. But there is also a common belief among Singaporean parents and teachers that homework nurtures discipline and good study habits—traits that they think will help students gain success in school and in life. When given in a reasonable and appropriate amount, homework can reinforce students' learning and contribute to their progress. However, in contrast with Finland's much shorter homework hours per week, it seems that a lot of homework does not necessarily translate to better education. In fact, according to an analysis of PISA results, the average number of hours that students spend on homework tends to be unrelated to the school system's overall performance. This implies that other factors, such as the quality of instruction and how schools are organised, have a greater impact on a school system's overall performance.[18]

In Singapore, not many people will dispute the importance of homework and getting children to practice what they learn, even if it is practicing on a worksheet rather than in real life. The question is really a matter of how much is enough and how much is too much. So, instead of giving more homework, in the spirit of 'Teach Less, Learn More', schools are working towards improving the quality of homework that is given. Quality here is twofold. First, homework should encourage students to study beyond rote learning and memorisation. In the words of a secondary school student,[19]

> My friends and I do complain, and I wish we had less homework, but
> we bear with it. Sometimes, doing the same type of questions gets quite

meaningless. But I enjoy the kind of homework that prompts me to do research and learn more.

Second, homework should be coordinated among subjects so that students are not overwhelmed. Jing Shan Primary School and Ahmad Ibrahim Primary Secondary School, for example, coordinate homework across subjects by installing a homework board at the back of their classrooms where homework, tests and projects in a given week or month are listed.[20] Furthermore, the schools track individual progress among students by updating their individual pupil handbook daily to communicate with parents about the list of homework students are assigned per day. This also helps students track their progress and take responsibility in managing their time spent on homework. Other schools have taken concrete steps to ease pressure on the students by reducing homework loads for their students. For example, Anglo-Chinese School (Junior) implemented homework-free days on Mondays and Thursdays, while River Valley High School developed a school-initiated homework ceiling policy of two hours per week.[21]

Stress from Extra Tuition

Shadow education is big business in Singapore (estimated to be a billion Singapore dollars a year). Paradoxically, while many parents are concerned with the long school hours and high pressure for their children, the private tuition industry is thriving because there is a demand for it from parents. Former Senior Minister of State for Education Indranee Rajah said in Parliament in 2013 that the education system was run on the basis that tuition was not necessary. Tuition for well-performing children, she said, could in fact be counter-productive, because it could create unnecessary stress, make them bored in class and take time away from other learning activities for holistic development. Also, she felt that weaker students could go for remedial and supplementary classes in schools or community schemes for help.[22] But some parents and students felt differently. They said tuition had an integral role in a system that emphasised academic excellence. Tuition was needed to maintain a competitive edge in school.[23]

Some students felt that private tuition helped them maintain focus and discipline in their studies. For others, tuition lessons compensated for the limited personal attention they received in class, given the relatively large class size in Singapore (30 to 40 students in a class). When interviewed, a Secondary 4 student who spent seven hours every week on tuition in four subjects said that "in school, the teachers' attention is divided. In tuition, the attention is concentrated on a few students so it's more focused". But this student was scoring good grades in school. So why did she need extra tuition? She explained that "tuition is useful, especially for math because I'm given a lot of extra worksheets to practice and reinforce concepts, in addition to what we do in school".[24]

Of course, there are also those who 'genuinely' need extra help to pass examinations, particularly in their weakest subjects. One student who used to fail science, mathematics and principles of accounting in secondary school, and who was now aiming for distinctions after her parents hired a private tutor for each subject for her, said:[25]

> Science was like Greek to me. I hated it because I'm more of an arts person . . . Tuition helped to bridge that gap and I got to clarify my doubts with the tutors . . . I like to ask a lot of questions, so to have a tutor who can answer all my questions without me being ridiculed is good.

Whatever the reasons or motivation may be, extra tuition adds to the load of a student. While some parents claim their children 'lose their childhood' through examination pressures, the same parents are probably sending their children for extra lessons to secure their grades. In fact, a newspaper reported that a small number of parents were paying for a private tutor to come to their homes, not for tuition lessons, but for the tutor to do their children's homework! Their children were struggling to cope with school assignments, co-curricular activities and extra work from tuition. Some private tutors were even hired to complete homework assigned not by the school teacher but by tuition centres! But, strangely, the parents persisted in sending their children to tuition![26]

Tuition in Singapore is here to stay, at least for the foreseeable future. In a free country, the education system cannot deprive parents of the right to give their children extra help if they wish to. The question is whether long hours spent in tuition will engage or disengage students from learning. Also, there is an opportunity cost. The time for tuition could be better spent on other more beneficial activities. There may not be cram schools in Singapore that operate beyond midnight. But there is concern about the long term effects of a heavy workload and stress on children. Some students may not experience a wholesome childhood. Others may lose their love of lifelong learning.

Initiatives to Improve Student Engagement

Singapore students in general work hard and can do well in examinations. In a way, they *are* learning in school. Also, according to the OECD, 87.9% of Singapore students reported that they were happy in school, which was significantly higher than the Finnish percentage of 66.9% or the OECD average of 79.8%[27] (mentioned in Chapter 1). However, what Singapore is working towards is achieving real engaged learning among students so that they find learning meaningful and intrinsically rewarding. Singapore is now examining strategies to address this challenge.

Essentially, the direction is to design more interesting lessons and appropriate learning platforms to suit the different learning styles of students. Since the implementation of TLLM in 2005, there have been concerted efforts at exploring strategies to promote engaged learning. For example, in 2009, when the MOE conducted the Primary Education Review and Implementation (PERI) and the Secondary Education Review and Implementation (SERI), innovative programmes such as the Programme for Active Learning (PAL) and Strategies for English Language Learning and Reading (STELLAR) were launched to engage students at the primary level. PAL, implemented for all Primary 1 and 2 students, exposes students to different and interesting learning experiences in four domains: sports and games, outdoor education, performing arts and visual arts. Through these sorts of activities, students also learn socio-emotional competencies such as respecting others and responsible decision-making. In STELLAR, primary school students are motivated to read and learn through enjoyable shared reading and writing experiences. The students, for instance, come together to read a big book edition of an interesting storybook. They get to act out parts of the story and even create their own parallel stories. Through the process, the teacher gets the students to respond experientially to the storyline of the books while teaching various aspects of the language.

In secondary schools, the Applied Learning Programme (ALP) (mentioned in Chapter 7) connects knowledge and skills learned in school with authentic settings in society and industries. The ALP may be applied in many areas, including business, entrepreneurship, design, engineering, environmental science, health services, journalism and broadcasting. The Learning for Life Programme (LLP) provides students with experiential learning to develop their character and cultivate people skills. The LLP may be applied in many areas too, including outdoor adventure, sports, uniformed groups, and performing and visual arts. These help students develop a stronger engagement with school and higher motivation to learn, because they now appreciate the direct relevance of what they are learning in the curriculum and apply that learning in real life.

The MOE not only encourages schools to be innovative in teaching and learning to engage students but also publishes resource books to share good ideas and practices among schools. A few examples from one of MOE's resource books illustrate the efforts of Singapore schools in engaging students in learning.[28] At Bendemeer Primary School, mathematical concepts are taught using a storybook approach. This initiative is an eight-week module with five lesson packages. The idea is that by using stories, children learn to understand the context and intent of the word problem to be solved, and they become more motivated to solve the problem. Mathematical concepts such as addition or multiplication are taught using various vocabularies associated with each concept. Numerals are gradually introduced through the characters and the plot of the story. Students are also encouraged to paraphrase or act out word problems, thereby building on vocabulary associated with mathematical concepts. Students also keep journals that help them write questions, sequence story plots and contextually situate mathematical problems. Solving word problems then becomes enjoyable to them. After the implementation of the programme, teachers noted a positive impact on student engagement in learning math concepts and student motivation in improving their word problem solving skills.

At Dunman Secondary School, the teachers implemented a school-based curriculum innovation called Music, English Language, and Literature (MEL). Initially part of the school's TLLM Ignite! project,

MEL is a 15-week programme for Dunman's Secondary 1 students which culminates in a performance art production or a musical. The programme aims at developing students' oral communication, collaborative, critical thinking and creative thinking skills. In the MEL, the learning of literature, music and English language is integrated. Through a production, the students are required to create, interpret and evaluate different scenarios that can be pieced together into one big project that they can call their own. Student assessment for MEL uses a detailed set of rubrics to assess the various skills in the three disciplines—English language, music, and literature. Weekly workbook activities help monitor student progress and guide them accordingly. English and music teachers immediately give feedback after every production. Students are required to write a reflection paper about the whole production process. Assessments are formative and carried out at various stages. After the implementation of the programme, students expressed an increased appreciation for music and literature. They developed greater resilience as they overcame production setbacks and negotiated with their peers or their teachers in their collaborative efforts. They demonstrated an increased confidence in public speaking, expressive speech and communication skills in the English language. The teachers also observed a greater sense of ownership among their students, as they were given various opportunities to take charge of their own learning.

These strategies can work for the average student. But what does a country do for students who are really struggling to keep up or really disengaged from academic learning? If every school is a good school, then there should be a good school for them as well. The solution, at the system level, to engage students who are not easily engaged in schools is to set up special secondary schools mentioned in Chapters 4 and 5. What differentiates these schools from others is the way they practice pedagogies that can engage students of that particular profile. Take Northlight School, for example. Established in 2007, this school takes in students who have failed their PSLE. To engage these learners, the teachers of the school have to teach differently:[29]

> We make our lessons authentic. There are opportunities for students to
> apply what they have learnt in class. We develop our own curriculum

and teaching packages and have moved away from using textbooks . . . Though many are not strong in Maths, they begin to experience the learning of it in a different and meaningful way. It's easier said than done but that's how we try to do it here.

The teachers work hard at understanding their students and making learning contextual and meaningful to them. How does one know that the students are more engaged in learning now? One simple indicator is how much these students want to attend school:[30]

> When the school was conceptualized, its target was to reduce the attrition rate from 60 per cent to 25 per cent. In NorthLight School, students are so motivated that the attrition rates of the graduating cohorts were 14 per cent in 2009 and only 10 per cent in 2011, outperforming the School's initial target of 25 per cent. Students feel a sense of belonging in NorthLight School. The hands-on pedagogy makes learning more interesting and they look forward to going to school.

These examples illustrate an important point. Innovations in teaching and learning are based on a better understanding of how students learn so that pedagogies may be tailored accordingly. Therefore, the effort to engage learners is not merely a 'creative' exercise for teachers to inject fun or novelty. The effort needs to be highly scientific as well. In this regard, Singapore is also developing research capabilities in the science of learning. In particular, as I have mentioned in Chapter 6, the Singapore National Research Foundation (NRF) supports research projects with generous funding to develop a scientific understanding of the effectiveness of Singapore's education methods and develop new methods to achieve better learning among students. The idea is to understand better how different students learn so that pedagogies may be tailored accordingly. The projects are meant to bring about the development of cognitive theories and interventions based on neuro-scientific evidence. These interventions also include the development of technological platforms and tools to support the scaling up of interventions. At the National Institute of Education, there are also numerous research projects in this area. Singapore aims to be a research hub in the area of learning sciences in the future.

Conclusion

In the 1990s, I was teaching mathematics to students who were at the age of 17–18. I had a chat with a few teachers in the cafeteria and a few were complaining that it was difficult to get students to be interested in learning anything that would not be examined. There was a lack of intellectual curiosity and spirit of exploration.

When I returned to the staff room, a student approached me with her 10-year series (a book compiling the national examination questions for the past 10 years). "Teacher, I don't understand this question. Could you please explain it to me?" I looked at her. Her brow was tightened. She looked highly perplexed and stressed. I looked at the offending question. Ah! It was one of those oldies from the 1970s. It would not be tested in the 1990s. I said, "Relax, it is not in the syllabus. I have not taught you this before. That's why you do not know how to do it."

Her expression was one of great relief. "Not in the syllabus? No wonder I could not do it." Then it turned to disgust. "I wasted the whole morning trying to work it out!" I said, "Well, it is actually quite interesting. If you want to know how it works . . ." I was about to go into my explanation when she said quickly, "No need, no need. This will not be tested in the examinations, right?" I nodded. "Don't waste time on this question. You haven't got much time before the exam." Again, she looked very relieved, presumably because she was spared a mathematics lecture.

She went out of the staff room a much happier student. I smiled, satisfied that I had helped a student in a small way. I began sorting out some papers. Then it struck me. What did I just say? Not in the syllabus? Don't waste time on this question? Weren't those things exactly what the teachers were complaining about? Teachers in Singapore have perhaps become so caught up in completing the syllabus, getting the students to get good results, that they have forgotten the importance of inculcating intellectual curiosity and a spirit of exploration. But the future belongs to a generation of creative and entrepreneurial people. This is still our challenge today.

References

1 Heng, S. K. (2012, September 12). Keynote Address by Mr Heng Swee Keat, Minister for Education at the Ministry of Education Work Plan Seminar at Ngee Ann Polytechnic Convention Centre. Retrieved from

http://www.moe.gov.sg/media/speeches/2012/09/12/keynote-address-by-mr-heng-swee-keat-at-wps-2012.php

2 Lee, H. L. (2004). *Let's Shape Our Future Together*. Swearing in Speech by Prime Minister Lee Hsien Loong. Retrieved from http://www.mfa.gov.sg/content/mfa/overseasmission/tokyo/press_statements_speeches/2004/200408/press_200408_5.html

3 Jones, B., Valdez, G., Nowakowski, J., & Rasmussen, C. (1994). *Designing Learning and Technology for Educational Reform*. Oak Brook: North Central Regional Educational Laboratory.

4 Luo, S. (2013, July 31). Cut some slack, give homework a rest. *The Straits Times*, p. A25.

5 Isralowitz, R. E. & Ong, T. H. (1990). Singapore youth: The impact of social status on perceptions of adolescent problems. *Adolescence*, 25(98), 357–362; Ho, K. C. & Yip, J. (2003). *YOUTH.sg: The State of Youth in Singapore*. Singapore: National Youth Council.

6 Ministry of Education (MOE) (2013, July 19). Highlights from Education Dialogue Session with Students. Retrieved from http://www.moe.gov.sg/our-singapore-conversation/files/highlights-students-dialogue-20130719.pdf

7 Huan, V. S., Yeo, L. S., Ang, R. P., & Chong, W. H. (2008). The impact of adolescent concerns on their academic stress. *Educational Review*, 60(2), 169–178.

8 Ministry of Education (MOE) (2013, July 19). Highlights from Education Dialogue Session with Students. Retrieved from http://www.moe.gov.sg/our-singapore-conversation/files/highlights-students-dialogue-20130719.pdf

9 Lee, P. (2015, February 7). Pupils get to hone skills with past years' PSLE papers. *The Straits Times*, p. B2.

10 Mokhtar, F. (2015, February 7). High demand for past PSLE papers. *Today Online*. Retrieved from http://www.todayonline.com/singapore/high-demand-past-psle-papers

11 Oon, L. (2013, June 6). June break packed with homework. *My Paper*, p. A10.

12 Huan, V. S., Yeo, L. S., Ang, R. P., & Chong, W. H. (2008). The impact of adolescent concerns on their academic stress. *Educational Review*, 60(2), 169–178.

13 Organization for Economic Cooperation and Development (OECD) (2014). *Does Homework Perpetuate Inequities in Education? PISA in Focus, Issue 46 (December)*. Paris: PISA, OECD Publishing.

14 Organization for Economic Cooperation and Development (OECD) (2014). *Does Homework Perpetuate Inequities in Education? PISA in Focus, Issue 46 (December)*. Paris: PISA, OECD Publishing.

15 Teng, A. (2014, December 25). S'pore ranks third globally in time spent on homework. *The Straits Times*, p. A6.

16 Teng, A. (2014, December 25). She takes 13 hours of homework a week in her stride. *The Straits Times*, p. A6.

17 Kua, J. (2013, September 14). Resolve unhealthy stress in school. *The Straits Times*, p. A35; Luo, S. (2013, July 31). Cut some slack, give homework a rest. *The Straits Times*, p. A25.

18 Organization for Economic Cooperation and Development (OECD) (2014). *Does Homework Perpetuate Inequities in Education? PISA in Focus, Issue 46 (December)*. Paris: PISA, OECD Publishing.

19 Teng, A. (2014, December 25). S'pore ranks third globally in time spent on homework. *The Straits Times*, p. A6.

20 Teng, A. (2014, December 25). S'pore ranks third globally in time spent on homework. *The Straits Times*, p. A6.

21 Toh, K. & Sim, B. (2012, September 14). Schools taking steps to reduce homework. *The Straits Times*, p. B2.

22 Rajah, I. (2013, September 16). Effects of Tuition on Mainstream Education. Parliamentary Replies by Senior Minister of State of Education, Indranee Rajah. Retrieved from http://www.moe.gov.sg/media/parliamentary-replies/2013/09/effects-of-tuition-on-mainstream-education.php

23 Teng, A. (2013, September 19). No tuition? No way, say some. *The Straits Times*, p. B6.

24 Teng, A. (2013, September 19). Tuition in four subjects despite doing well. *The Straits Times*, p. B6.

25 Teng, A. (2013, September 19). From failing science, she now aims to ace it. *The Straits Times*, p. B6.

26 Humphries, H. (2015, April 13). Kids sleep, private tutors do their homework. *The New Paper*, p. 4.

27 Organization for Economic Cooperation and Development (OECD) (2013). *PISA 2012 Results: Ready to Learn: Students' Engagement, Drive and Self-Beliefs* (Volume 3). Paris: PISA, OECD Publishing.

28 Ministry of Education (MOE) (2013). *Engaging our Learners: Teach Less, Learn More*. Singapore: Ministry of Education.

29 Lie, E. (2013). NorthLight School—Giving less academically inclined students hope. *EduNation issue 6*. Retrieved from http://www.edunationsg.com/2013/201306/cover-story02.html#.UpcCRtIW18E

30 Lie, E. (2013). NorthLight School—Giving less academically inclined students hope. *EduNation issue 6*. Retrieved from http://www.edunationsg.com/2013/201306/cover-story02.html#.UpcCRtIW18E

9

DREAM 3

Every Teacher, a Caring Educator

Teachers are in a profession where the heart matters as much, if not more, than the mind. No matter how governments may change the education system in terms of its structure, curriculum, assessment, and examination, quality education does not happen unless there are caring teachers to deliver it. An education system without caring teachers is like a car without fuel. What is a caring teacher? Minister Heng Swee Keat said:[1]

> A caring teacher is one who believes that every child can learn, and acts on that belief. He is able to connect with and motivate the child—know the child, shape the child's values and character, help the child grow as a person and bring out the best in the child. A caring teacher is also a skillful teacher—one who masters her content, and is able to engage students through thoughtful planning and skillful execution. I know it is not easy to be a caring teacher.

So, there are two aspects to being a caring teacher. The first is an affective aspect—a caring teacher cares about his or her students, so that they grow up well. The second is a professional aspect—a caring teacher cares about his or her craft, so that he or she may teach the students well.

Successful education systems share a common success factor of maintaining high teacher standards.[2] In various publications, the factor of high quality teachers has been cited as a key reason for the high level of performance of the Singapore education system.[3] Singapore has a highly selective and rigorous process of teacher recruitment, choosing applicants only from the top 30% of their academic cohort.

Prospective teachers are interviewed so that only those who are genuinely interested in teaching are recruited. Tuition fees for teacher training are fully covered by the MOE and a salary is paid during teacher training! The starting salary is comparable to other prestigious professions such as engineering and law, and there are different development and career advancement tracks for teachers. Teachers can advance on one of the three tracks—teaching, leadership and specialist—depending on their strength and aptitude. Each track comes with attractive service terms and developmental opportunities. Teachers are respected in Singapore, much more than in the United States or United Kingdom. Teachers are well paid (in fact, they received 4–9% salary increase in 2015) and have stable jobs. They have good career prospects. Essentially, Singapore's teacher recruitment, preparation, professional development and career pathways have all contributed to its highly effective education system. What seems to be the lesson to be learned here? Pay teachers well? Treat teachers well? I agree. But there is more to the story.

Singapore recognises something that not too many education systems in the world recognise. It is said that it takes a village to raise a child. In the same way, it takes a community of professionals to sustain a caring teacher. Caring is not just a feeling. It is a continuous giving of self, both emotionally and in action. Many teachers feel stress in their work, as they face complex challenges in dealing with both the professional and emotional aspects of their work. Many people join the teaching profession with the heart to serve. They leave when they are exhausted or disillusioned. Therefore, as challenges become more complex, Singapore is mindful that the Singapore education service has to evolve to help teachers care and continue to care! It is unrealistic to expect teachers to care for their students and their craft on their own, without support from the system, or worse, when they are shackled by the system.

Many people have watched movies of inspiring teachers, like *Dead Poets Society*. There is usually a feel-good factor at the end of the movie. Inspiring teachers inspire because fundamentally they care. They care enough for their students to connect with them, shape them skillfully and give them hope for a better future. But, in the movies, caring teachers are often portrayed as lone heroes. They are individuals who go against an uncaring system or school, motivating children to beat the odds while battling heartless or mindless leaders and authorities. They are the mavericks. They are the daring ones. Their actions are based only on their own personality or convictions. Their students are lucky to have them as teachers. This may be well and good in the movies, but this will not do in Singapore.

A small country where every child counts does not leave it to chance whether children meet a caring teacher. 'Every Teacher, a Caring Educator' expresses the ideal of a teaching profession. One sees the true mark of a quality teaching force when one sees teachers who care passionately about students and education throughout the country. This is not just about an individual teacher. This is about a system. Singapore teachers care as individuals. They also care as a community of professionals. Caring is an individual effort and also a systemic one. The Singapore education system pays attention to ensuring that teachers are supported to be caring educators. Minister Heng said that "to have teachers who care, we must care for our teachers".[4] There are therefore three important aspects of the way Singapore promotes teachers as caring educators:

- *Affective.* Support teachers to care about their students.
- *Professional.* Support teachers to care about their craft.
- *Systemic.* Support caring teachers to continue to care.

As we further explore this, let us first understand the challenges of a Singapore teacher.

Challenges of a Singapore Teacher

Teachers are required to take on multiple roles. Throughout their careers they are coaches, mentors, and role models to their students. Beyond being efficient and effective transmitters of knowledge and facilitators of learning, teachers must aspire to be affective educators. What motivates teachers to be caring educators is their passion—for their craft, for their students, for their moral stance on the value of education and its transforming powers for every human being. It is by no means an easy feat to be a caring teacher.

Some teachers, if not many of them, feel drained by the daily demands in their teaching lives. They are good teachers, wanting to do their best. But given the daily grind, they feel like a flickering candle, not completely gone but hardly burning anymore. Each year, there are many fresh-faced beginning teachers, all eager to become the inspiring teacher they hope to be. But at the end of a few years, many have lost steam. They do care. Deep down, they care a lot. But it is tough. Being a teacher is a lot more than just teaching a subject in a classroom. It is tough taking care of so many students. Amidst the daily teaching in the classroom, teachers have numerous responsibilities and commitments to attend to. These include meeting parents, counselling problematic students, participating in school projects, attending committee meetings, running extra-curricular activities and of course marking students' work and preparing lessons. The list appears endless. Ask a few teachers in Singapore about their daily schedule in school and they will express how demanding a typical school day can be.

The wife of one teacher at a neighbourhood school wrote to a local newspaper regarding her husband's long hours of work and expressed her concerns about the lack of work-life balance resulting from such demanding work:[5]

> Weekends are hardly restful. I often ask him if the endless work is because he is singled out. That is not so, he tells me. His colleagues face the same punishing workload. As I am writing this letter at 10 a.m., my husband has developed a fever. But he is unable to seek medical attention as there is an oral examination in the afternoon. I understand there is a need to be accountable to students' parents. But in this case, who is answerable to a teacher's family if anything happens to the teacher?

Teachers often lament that, with the high volume of classroom and non-classroom duties they must fulfil, something will eventually have to give way. According to a newspaper report, a former school teacher said that lesson planning and preparation took a backseat as teachers became too preoccupied with attending to logistical concerns in fulfilling their administrative responsibilities. The important process of reflective teaching became second priority. There was too much 'noise' in the daily life of a teacher to find a quiet moment for reflection.[6]

According to the 2013 Teaching and Learning International Survey (TALIS), Singapore teachers work an average of 48 hours a week—10 hours more than the survey average. They actually spend less time on classroom teaching (17 hours a week, compared with the survey average of 19), but significantly more time on marking or administrative tasks compared with teachers in other countries.[7] Even when the survey results indicated that Singapore teachers were some of the most hard-working teachers in the world, some teachers were skeptical of the results. When interviewed by the media, they indicated that 48 hours a week was hardly the average number but rather the minimum of the number of hours they normally had to work in a week. They indicated that 50 hours would be a more accurate figure for the average. The teachers cited several reasons for such long hours. Class size in Singapore averages 36 students compared to the global average of 24. Singapore teachers have to teach multiple classes, and they spend a considerable amount of time marking students' homework and attending to administrative work.[8] Teachers also provide remediation for weaker students, set and mark school examinations, handle co-curricular activities and other programmes for the holistic development of students, as well as devote time to pastoral care and parent engagement.

Caring is especially challenging when a teacher teaches many students in a year. It is tough to give personalised attention to every student. Singapore stresses the importance of teachers seizing teachable moments to impart values to students. It is hard to preach values through a lesson. A teachable moment provides the context for students to relate to values directly and meaningfully. But it takes a teacher who cares enough to seize every teachable moment, especially when it is out of the regular classroom hours. A few teachers told me that they had knowingly allowed some teachable moments to slip by them because they were too exhausted to handle one more student. A teacher told me, "I do care, but don't I have enough to handle already? It is not easy to be a caring teacher!" Even Minister Heng acknowledged, "Teaching is not a nine-to-five job . . . the more caring our educators, the more stressed they feel".[9]

After the release of the TALIS 2013 report, one local newspaper asserted, "Teachers in Singapore more respected than in Finland, UK, US".[10] But most teachers probably feel differently. The reality is that the dynamics in student-teacher interaction are increasingly complex. Many experienced teachers lament the fact that the good old era of having disciplined and respectful students has gone. Student discipline is deteriorating. Children these days are too preoccupied with technological distractions, thereby decreasing their opportunities to develop essential social skills. To some teachers, despite the best intentions of the education system, an era of cheeky, indolent and disruptive students, backed by over-protective parents who constantly threaten to complain to the principal or even the minister, has been ushered in. Cheeky, indolent and disruptive students may be in the minority rather than majority. But handling a few such cases each week can easily deplete a teacher's energy and motivation.

One newspaper report noted that parents had become increasingly demanding in recent years and that this had loaded emotional stress on teachers. According to the report, parents wanted to have a say in a range of matters, such as classroom management and teaching methods, and some had also confronted teachers or threatened to go to the media. Parents, on the other hand, said they just wanted the best for their children's education. The report also carried the views of a local sociologist, who felt that Singapore was becoming a more consumerist society in which parents and their children saw themselves as clients or customers, while teachers and the schools were service providers.[11]

Some teachers are understandably worried about over-protective parents who would like to bubble-wrap their children if possible. Because of the fear of how parents may escalate an issue, some teachers would rather err on the side of caution and give in on discipline issues.[12] Moreover, as Singapore progresses, many parents will have equal or higher qualifications than teachers. They are inclined to tell teachers what they think teachers should be doing for their child. The problem is that this may demoralise some teachers. Their teaching is affected and the students will be the eventual victims.

Minister Heng acknowledged that teachers had a very difficult task of managing vocal parents. He urged parents to give teachers their support and commented that students, parents and teachers had an integral role in upholding regard for the teaching profession.[13] The MOE has come out in support of teachers in handling discipline, indicating that it would stand by teachers who maintained discipline appropriately.[14] Even when high interactivity is encouraged in classrooms, students have to respect their teachers and be taught basic respect for other people. Otherwise, the learning environment in school will be compromised. In order that caring teachers may be supported enough to discipline and educate errant children appropriately, Singapore needs a collective understanding and effort from many parties. I remember a school leader sharing with me that if teachers feel that students and parents are engaging them respectfully in professional matters and problem solving, they will naturally be driven by their sense of mission to do what is best for their students. 'Every Teacher, a Caring Educator' is not a vision that can be achieved by the effort of teachers alone.

But while some parents may be too lenient with their own children's bad behaviour, the society always expects high moral standards from the teachers. In 2012, Singapore was shaken with a few scandals involving members of the teaching profession. One scandal involved a former school principal and was prominently featured in the news.[15] The general public is outraged by these scandals. Educators are entrusted to nurture and guide the children. Citizens expect only those who have the right moral values and character to take on this enormous responsibility. This is a reflection of Singapore society's high regard for and expectations of its educators. Minister Heng said:[16]

> From time-to-time, we do have teachers who do not live up to their high calling and who disappoint us. We must and will take cases of educators' misconduct seriously so as to maintain public trust. We must uphold the ethos and values of the profession so that it continues to command respect. The vast majority of educators uphold high professional standards and we must aspire to enable every teacher to be a caring and competent teacher.

So how does a country support every teacher to be a caring teacher?

Supporting Teachers as Caring Educators

Actually, Singapore teachers are generally very resilient. They may be stressed. They may complain about their heavy responsibilities among themselves. But they persist. In a parliamentary reply in 2013, MOE indicated that the annual resignation rate for teachers had remained low at around 3% over the past five years. Moreover, workload has not been cited as a major reason for resigning in exit interviews and surveys.[17] According to the TALIS 2013 survey, 88% of the teachers in Singapore are generally satisfied with their chosen vocation, not too far off the global average of 91%.[18] Even so, Singapore takes deliberate steps to support its teachers to be caring educators.

First, from a system perspective, the teaching force must be strong enough in numbers to match the volume of work to be done. So a direct and practical strategy is to increase the number of teachers. In 2010, there were 30,000 teachers. In 2015, this has increased to 33,000 teachers. This number is not expected to increase further in the short run. An Allied Educator Scheme and Relief Allied Educator Scheme were implemented to assist teachers in addressing behavioural and academic issues in schools and to provide short-term human resource support respectively. Minister Heng said:[19]

> Many of you (teachers) are torn between tending to your own children, and tending to your students who you care deeply for as well. We understand this and regularly review our Human Resource (HR) policies to better meet the needs of teachers for work-life balance. For example, as teachers do not have annual leave, we have provisions for teachers to go on urgent leave if necessary. For teachers who need to take longer absences beyond six months, MOE deploys up to 1,000 replacements at any one time to ensure that their duties are adequately covered.

Second, the education system supports teachers in their professional development. According to TALIS 2013, Singapore teachers are some of the best trained teachers in the world.[20] Ninety-eight percent undergo rigorous pre-service training in actual classroom practices before formally becoming a teacher (compared to the TALIS average of 89%). Ninety-eight percent participate in professional development activities (TALIS average 88%). Ninety-four percent collaborate in professional learning teams (TALIS average 84%). Eighty percent have participated in classroom observations and feedback exercises (TALIS average 55%). Thirty-nine percent serve as mentors (TALIS average 14%). Sixty-eight percent believe that the teaching profession is respected and valued in the Singapore society (TALIS average

31%). Singapore also has one of the most youthful teaching work-forces in the world. The average age of a Singapore teacher is 36 years old—7 years younger than the global average of 43 years old. Singapore also has the largest proportion of teachers who are below 30 years old.[21] The MOE attributes this to its deliberate and sustained teacher recruitment efforts, which rejuvenate and expand its teaching workforce.[22]

Third, the education system systematically supports teachers with the potential for higher level appointments to move forward in their career through various milestone programmes at the NIE.[23] For example, the Leaders in Education Programme (LEP) is a prestigious six-month full-time executive programme to prepare carefully selected vice-principals (or MOE officers at the equivalent level) for school leadership. The Management and Leadership in Schools (MLS) programme is a 17-week full-time executive programme for middle leaders of school who have been selected by their school leaders. In these programmes, the participants are encouraged to keenly reflect on their own educational philosophies and practices. They are also attached to schools (not the ones they come from) to undertake authentic projects that will add value to the school, especially in the areas of teaching and learning. These projects create the theory-practice nexus by involving participants in authentic situations and develop their leadership by requiring them to lead in school-based projects without formal position or authority. Participants in these programmes are fully sponsored by the MOE. They receive their regular salary during the programme. They also go on an overseas learning trip (2 weeks for LEP, 1 week for MLS; fully sponsored by MOE) so that they may observe a different system and allow those observations to trigger them to reflect on their own ideas for change.

Fourth, in Singapore, there is a deliberate effort to remind teachers of the roles, purposes, values and ethos of the teaching profession, and to draw strength from within. At the National Institute of Education (NIE), where all teachers are trained, the enhanced V^3SK model (Values, Skills, and Knowledge) is the current teacher training framework. The 'Values' concept is central to the model and is made up three strands to emphasise learner-centredness, teacher identity, and service to the profession and community.[24] Every teacher in Singapore takes the Teachers' Pledge. This pledge, shown below, is recited annually at the investiture ceremony for teachers, led usually by the director general of education, after they have undergone teacher training at the NIE:[25]

> We, the teachers of Singapore, pledge that:
>> We will be true to our mission to bring out the best in our students.
>> We will be exemplary in the discharge of our duties and responsibilities.
>> We will guide our students to be good and useful citizens of Singapore.
>> We will continue to learn and pass on the love of learning to our students.
>> We will win the trust, support and co-operation of parents and the
> community so as to enable us to achieve our mission.

Newly qualified teachers are presented with a compass at the Teachers' Compass Ceremony. The compass, which points to the true north, depicts the various facets of the Ethos of the Teaching Profession and symbolises the constancy of teachers' values.[26] This is the expectation for a Singapore teacher. The pledge and the compass are reminders to teachers of their roles and responsibilities. The strength of the Singapore system lies not just in the individual teachers, but in the community of teachers, working conscientiously, day in and day out, across the whole nation. The whole is greater than the sum of the parts. Therefore, Singapore does a lot to build the teaching community and for the community to support one another, recognising that it is hard to be a caring teacher.

Fifth, in Singapore, there is a deliberate effort to care for teachers and protect the image of the teaching profession. Each year, Singapore celebrates Teachers' Day. On this day, throughout Singapore, students pay tributes to their teachers in a very heartwarming way. Many students make cards for their teachers. Others put up performances. There is also the prestigious annual President's Award for Teachers (PAT), which is Singapore's highest accolade that honours outstanding and caring teachers who are dedicated to nurturing and inspiring their students. Launched in 1998, three or four teachers are given the award each year. At the Istana, which is the official presidential residence and office, the President will personally confer the award to the recipients on Teachers' Day. The MOE has also created a website that allows students or parents to send their appreciation to their teachers.

The website is entitled "Your Words of Encouragement". Teachers are able to view compliments online and gain emotional support to carry on their good work.

On some public buses in Singapore, you will see large advertisements reminding the public that education is 'Moulding the Future of the Nation'. The MOE also launches commercials on television, educating the citizens of the great mission carried out by teachers. The TV commercials, such as those featuring 'Mrs Chong', 'Mrs Cordeiro' and 'Mr Kumar', won the praise and tears of many citizens (and even viewers' choice awards for TV commercials) because they depicted how a caring teacher could help turn around a student who otherwise would have been lost in life. These may be the stories of great teachers in Singapore, but the work of the average teacher in Singapore is the same—perhaps just less 'dramatic'.

The MOE, in solidarity with the teachers, has also created a website called Schoolbag (https://schoolbag.sg/) which publishes real life stories of the interaction between teachers and students that have a positive impact on the students. Such stories uplift the image and morale of the teachers as well as celebrate their successes with the entire society. Let's highlight one such story that ties in with the commercial featuring 'Mr Kumar'.[27]

For some time in 2013, there was a TV commercial aired on the local TV network about a teacher named Mr Kumar and his student Glenn. Each segment of the commercial showed young Glenn in a type of trouble—with his family, in school and even in a brush with the law. At the end of each segment, one sees Mr Kumar disciplining and advising Glenn. The commercial ends with Glenn, who is now a youth specialist consultant working with community agencies focusing on youth outreach and rehabilitation, expressing his gratitude to Mr Kumar. Glenn shared how his experiences with a caring teacher like Mr Kumar changed his life.

> Mr Kumar has a different approach when it comes to dealing with difficult students. I was one of them. When people around seemed to have lost confidence in me, Mr Kumar stood firm, and maintained his authority when dealing with me. Despite that, he was neither demeaning nor condescending. Although Mr Kumar was disappointed with me

at times, he gave me room to redeem myself. Always encouraging me to take small steps towards changing my behaviour for the better, he never lost patience in guiding me. Mr Kumar restored me to who I am today.

As the case of Glenn and Mr Kumar shows, a caring teacher can have a lasting impact on the lives of his or her students. Sharing his experiences as a teacher for 36 years, Mr Kumar explained his philosophy of helping students in trouble:

> It is a question of making pupils reflect on the choices that they make and the subsequent consequences. If I can convince them to take responsibility for their choices, the battle is already half won. The other half is to get them to work out solutions to their problems and how I can be instrumental in helping them.

What gave Mr Kumar satisfaction?

> I know this sounds like a cliché, but when you hear your students and ex-students tell you (sometimes years later) that you had impacted them in one way or another and that you had made a difference in their lives, it makes your day and makes teaching as a career all the more meaningful.

Other than teachers building students, Singapore also believes in teachers building teachers. Take another story from the Schoolbag website. Mr Muhamad Salahuddin Bin Ibrahim is Lead Teacher (Biology) at Serangoon Junior College. He leads the way as a tireless mentor to new and experienced teachers. He hopes to create communities of teachers who fearlessly share and learn from one another. He says:[28]

> Since 2008, I have thoroughly enjoyed mentoring about four new teachers every year by giving them advice, observing them in class and helping them to hone their craft. A common issue they face is how to ensure that their students do not just enjoy lessons, but really understand what is being taught . . . I enjoy sharing what I know, because there is power in collaboration . . . This collaboration, if taken to a national level, can truly uplift the profession. That is why I work closely with the Academy of Singapore Teachers to run workshops at a national level, for it enables me to help teachers beyond my college. It is through these workshops that I have gotten to know teachers from other schools, who have called on me to mentor them or help them with research projects.

These stories on Schoolbag are not mere stories. They signify how important teachers are in Singapore. They encourage and build Singapore's teachers.

Conclusion

In the 1990s, when I was teaching students of the age 17–18, a class of mine decided to go to town for dinner after school. I joined them. We boarded a bus and sat down somewhere at the front of the bus. My students were evidently in high spirits. They joked, laughed and made the environment in the bus, which was quiet before we boarded, rather noisy. The bus driver might have had a bad day. He turned around to my students and hurled some abuse at them. Then he spat, "What school are you all from? Who is your stupid teacher? He did not teach you all to shut up?"

To be fair, my students were not really behaving in an unruly manner. They were a bit on the noisy side, but definitely more civilised in language compared to the torrent of abusive verbs and adjectives from the driver himself. A few students, especially the boys, sat up and looked as though they were about to retaliate, at least in language. I stopped them. One guy was indignant. "But it's so unfair! We didn't do anything! He is throwing bad language at us. We are not afraid of him." He had a point. The rest nodded. I told them, "But we were noisy. We could have been more considerate. So the driver had a point. Let's be quiet. He shouted abuse at us. You all felt that that was not civilised. You would like to confront him. Is that more civilised?"

I walked up to the bus driver, who cast a half-wary, half-belligerent glance in my direction. I said, "We are sorry to make so much noise. I am their teacher and I am sorry that I have not taught my students well." For a comical moment, I was quite sure he did not know how to respond. Perhaps he was expecting a challenge. Maybe he thought I was a student as well. He certainly did not expect the 'stupid' teacher to appear and apologise to him. He spluttered, "It's OK . . . I mean students are always noisy . . . not that they are bad . . . sorry . . . I mean . . . I mean . . ." I got what he meant. I chatted with him a bit more about his day. He told me all about students crowding the bus, especially in the evening, making lots of noise and refusing to cooperate with him by moving to the rear of the bus. Ah, the source of his frustrations. I returned to my students. They were all eager to know what had transpired between the driver and me. I told them. Some looked amused. Others looked intrigued. I told them, "True strength is not how you can get back at others who have offended you. It takes strength to be gentle."

When our destination came, I walked up to the driver to say goodbye to him. He specifically opened the front entrance for me to get down even when there was no one wanting to get onto the bus. If you knew the bus driver culture in Singapore, you would know that that was a very special gesture of friendship. This was an episode that happened many years ago. Today, as Singapore emphasises values education in an increasing complex world, teachers have to seize teachable moments even more. A teacher who cares seizes every opportunity to teach his students. An education system that cares seizes every opportunity to build its teachers.

References

1 Heng, S. K. (2012, September 12). Keynote Address by Mr Heng Swee Keat, Minister for Education at the Ministry of Education Work Plan Seminar at Ngee Ann Polytechnic Convention Centre. Retrieved from http://www.moe.gov.sg/media/speeches/2012/09/12/keynote-address-by-mr-heng-swee-keat-at-wps-2012.php

2 Darling-Hammond, L. (2010). Teacher education and the American future. *Journal of Teacher Education*, 61(1–2), 35–47; Mourshed, M., Chijioke, C., & Barber, M. (2010). *How the World's Most Improved School Systems Keep Getting Better*. London: McKinsey.

3 Read, for example, Darling-Hammond, L. & Rothman, R. (2011). Lessons learned from Finland, Ontario, and Singapore. In L. Darling-Hammond & R. Rothman (Eds.), *Teacher and Leader Effectiveness in High-Performing Education Systems* (pp. 1–12). Washington, DC: Alliance for Excellent Education and Stanford, CA: Stanford Center for Opportunity Policy in Education; Goodwin, A. L. (2012). Quality teachers, Singapore style. In L. Darling-Hammond & A. Lieberman (Eds.), *Teacher Education Around the World: Changing Policies and Practices* (pp. 22–43). New York: Routledge; Sclafani, S. (2008). *Rethinking Human Capital in Education: Singapore as a Model for Teacher Development*. Washington, DC: Aspen Institute.

4 Heng, S. K. (2012, September 12). Keynote Address by Mr Heng Swee Keat, Minister for Education at the Ministry of Education Work Plan Seminar at Ngee Ann Polytechnic Convention Centre. Retrieved from

http://www.moe.gov.sg/media/speeches/2012/09/12/keynote-address-by-mr-heng-swee-keat-at-wps-2012.php

5 Quek, A. (2012, May 5). Work-life balance? Here's one day in the life of a teacher. *The Straits Times*, p. A42.

6 Teng, A. (2014, June 27). "48 hours? It's more than that", says teachers. *The Straits Times*, p. B14.

7 Organization for Economic Cooperation and Development (OECD) (2014). *TALIS 2013 Results: An International Perspective on Teaching and Learning*. Paris: OECD Publishing.

8 Teng, A. (2014, June 27). "48 hours? It's more than that", says teachers. *The Straits Times*, p. B14.

9 Heng, S. K. (2012, September 12). Keynote Address by Mr Heng Swee Keat, Minister for Education at the Ministry of Education Work Plan Seminar at Ngee Ann Polytechnic Convention Centre. Retrieved from http://www.moe.gov.sg/media/speeches/2012/09/12/keynote-address-by-mr-heng-swee-keat-at-wps-2012.php

10 Today (2013, October 3). Teachers in Singapore more respected than in Finland, UK, US: Study. *Today Online*. Retrieved from http://www.today-online.com/daily-focus/education/teachers-singapore-more-respected-finland-uk-us-study

11 Ng, J. Y. (2012, June 8). Teachers feel more heat from parents. *Today*, p. 1.

12 Ho, K. L. (2010, August 12). Where's the discipline?—Too often, school leaders' hands are tied when dealing with errant students. *Today*, p. 12.

13 Ng, J. Y. (2012, June 8). Teachers feel more heat from parents. *Today*, p. 1.

14 Ministry of Education (MOE) (2010, August 18). Discipline Is Key. Forum Letter Replies. Retrieved from http://www.moe.gov.sg/media/forum/2010/08/discipline-is-key.php

15 Chan, F. & Chong, E. (2012, April 28). Ex-principal jailed 9 weeks. *The Straits Times*, p. A3.

16 Heng, S. K. (2012, September 12). Keynote Address by Mr Heng Swee Keat, Minister for Education at the Ministry of Education Work Plan Seminar at Ngee Ann Polytechnic Convention Centre. Retrieved from http://www.moe.gov.sg/media/speeches/2012/09/12/keynote-address-by-mr-heng-swee-keat-at-wps-2012.php

17 Ministry of Education (MOE) (2013, November 11). Teacher Workload and Resignation Rate. Parliamentary Replies. Retrieved from http://www.moe.gov.sg/media/parliamentary-replies/2013/11/Teacher%20workload%20and%20resignation%20rate.php

18 Organization for Economic Cooperation and Development (OECD) (2014). *TALIS 2013 Results: An International Perspective on Teaching and Learning*. Paris: OECD Publishing; Organization for Economic Cooperation and Development (OECD) (2014). *Singapore: Country note—Results from TALIS 2013*. Paris: OECD Publishing.

19 Heng, S. K. (2012, September 12). Keynote Address by Mr Heng Swee Keat, Minister for Education at the Ministry of Education Work Plan Seminar at Ngee Ann Polytechnic Convention Centre. Retrieved from

http://www.moe.gov.sg/media/speeches/2012/09/12/keynote-address-by-mr-heng-swee-keat-at-wps-2012.php

20 Organization for Economic Cooperation and Development (OECD) (2014). *TALIS 2013 Results: An International Perspective on Teaching and Learning*. Paris: OECD Publishing.

21 Organization for Economic Cooperation and Development (OECD) (2014). *TALIS 2013 Results: An International Perspective on Teaching and Learning*. Paris: OECD Publishing.

22 Ministry of Education (MOE) (2014, June 25). International OECD Study Shows a Quality, Dynamic and Committed Teaching Force in Singapore. Press Release. Retrieved from http://www.moe.gov.sg/media/press/2014/06/international-oecd-study-shows-a-quality-dynamic-and-committed-teaching-force-in-singapore.php

23 Ng, P. T. (2013). Developing Singapore school leaders to handle complexity in times of uncertainty. *Asia Pacific Education Review*, 14(1), 67–73; Ng, P. T. (2015). Developing leaders for schools in Singapore. In A. Harris & M. Jones (Eds.), *Leading Futures—Global Perspectives on Educational Leadership* (pp. 162–176). New York: SAGE.

24 National Institute of Education (NIE) (2009). *TE21: A Teacher Education Model for the 21st Century*. Singapore: National Institute of Education.

25 Ministry of Education (MOE) (2013). *The Teachers' Pledge*. Retrieved from http://www.moe.gov.sg/about/

26 Academy of Singapore Teachers (AST) (2012). *Ethos of the Teaching Profession*. Retrieved from http://www.academyofsingaporeteachers.moe.gov.sg/professional-excellence/ethos-of-the-teaching-profession

27 Schoolbag (2013, February 19). Teachers Who Made a Difference—Mr. Kumar. Retrieved from http://schoolbag.sg/story/teachers-who-made-a-difference-mr-kumar

28 Schoolbag (2015, September 3). The Teacher's Teacher. Retrieved from https://schoolbag.sg/story/the-teacher-s-teacher#.VgPQhCEZ6po

10

DREAM 4

Every Parent, a Supportive Partner

A primary school child was caught by his teacher using expletives in communicating with other children. The teacher chastised the child. She told him that such language was offensive and should not be repeated. The teacher decided to inform the child's parents so that the parents could send the same message at home and help the child truly understand the inappropriateness of using expletives. When the child's father arrived in school and found out about his child's bad behaviour, he scolded his child—and he did so emphatically in front of the teacher, complete with expletives! Now the teacher realised where the child had learned the offensive language.

Children bring to school the things they observe and learn at home. Children of schooling age spend the majority of their day in school, but the parents, as primary givers of care and support for their children, undoubtedly have a great degree of influence in their children's lives. At a conference for Parent Support Groups, Minister Heng Swee Keat said that:[1]

> MOE shares the same hopes and dreams of every parent. All of us at MOE and in our schools are dedicated to bringing out the best in every child. MOE wants to bring out the best in every child, in every domain of learning, in every school, at every stage of the learning journey, whatever the starting point so that we can create a better future together. Today, I want to emphasise the word 'together'—We look forward to doing this with the active partnership of parents who care about the future of our children. Parents are important because you are your child's first and most important teacher in life.

It is said that it takes a village to raise a child. Singapore recognises this. The education system is not a stand-alone system. It is deeply entwined with the society. For education reform to work and be sustainable, policy makers and educators have to work with stakeholders outside the school system, especially the parents. Therefore, it is Singapore's dream to have every parent be a supportive partner in the schooling lives of their children. Trying to achieve this is of course a big challenge.

Issues and Challenges

Many Singapore students find education quite stressful. The question is, Where does all this pressure come from? A significant part of the pressure comes from their own parents. A desire for their children's academic success is part of a typical Singaporean parent's DNA. One can attribute it partially to the Confucian heritage culture in the Singaporean society.[2] But the parents are also conditioned through the history that Singapore has gone through. For a long time and even now, education is the key to a good life. As the common rhetoric goes, education is the leveler in society, and a good academic qualification is the key to upward social mobility. Parents may not start out with an intention to pressurise their children. They want the best for their children and hope that their children will have a better future than they had. It is all 'for their own good', and parents are sometimes blind to the unseen pressure. The current mindset that the majority of Singaporean parents still have is that the one secure route to success is a good degree from a prestigious university, which opens the doors to prosperity that will otherwise be shut.

Parents with Different Opinions

As parents become increasingly well educated, school leaders and teachers face parents with strong views about education. Prime Minister Lee Hsien Loong observed:[3]

> Whomever you are teaching, whatever your kids are like, you will need
> to work with the parents because nowadays, many parents take a very

close interest in how their kids are doing in schools, in the education of their children. And they not only have a close interest, they also have strong views about how their children should be taught, whether they have been taught right and wrong.

But parents are of course a diverse group of people. Different parents have different opinions of what good education is and how education should be run. As I have described in Chapter 3, a student's performance during the PSLE determines the course in which he or she will be placed in secondary school. Their results are measured in an aggregate T-score that emphasises performance relative to peers. This implies that a high score does not automatically ensure a spot in one's school of choice. It depends on the performances of the rest. In order to reduce competition and stress among students, the prime minister announced that the T-score system would be changed to a grade band system. The criteria for DSA would be broadened to include qualities like character and leadership, in the hope of recognising more areas of success and diversifying the secondary school landscape.

There has been a mixed reaction from various stakeholders about the changes on the PSLE and the DSA. For the PSLE scoring system, most people were supportive of it but curious as to how the new system would work. Others felt that basing PSLE results on broad grades instead of an absolute score could make it less meritocratic, more subjective and less transparent. The DSA changes worried some other parents, who raised questions such as, How do we determine good character in the admission process to good schools? Who will make this judgement and can this be done fairly? Should a kind act motivated by external recognition be judged as being the same as an act of compassion for others? How does one tell the difference? Will the DSA changes encourage children (or their parents) to view kindness as a transaction, doing good deeds for the sake of gain? Minister Heng acknowledged that this was indeed "a complex subject tied very much to our values and expectations as a society".[4] Different parents have different opinions. It is hard to please everyone or have a position that everyone can accept.

Kiasu *Parents*

Kiasu is a Singaporean colloquial term derived from the Chinese vernacular that literally means 'fear of losing'. When one is *kiasu*, one is afraid of losing out to someone else, sometimes to the point of being selfish or paranoid. For the most part, however, being *kiasu* means staying ahead of the game by taking extra preparatory measures or by grabbing the best opportunities possible.

Kiasu parenting seems to be the norm these days. It is a trait that is increasingly pronounced as Singapore becomes more competitive. Parent volunteerism in primary schools is a platform where the *kiasu* mentality among parents is manifested.[5] As I have described in Chapter 7, ideally parents volunteer to help schools because they are interested and see value in helping schools. To recognise them for their efforts, they get priority if they wish to send their children to the school they have volunteered in. However, nowadays, the volunteer scheme becomes a means for parents to secure their child's admission into a school of their choice. Popular schools get a long queue of parents wanting to volunteer their services. Not so popular ones have a shortage of parent volunteers, therefore making it even more difficult for them to gain the recognition they need to attract students. Although some form of recognition for parent volunteers is important, parent volunteerism should not be a transaction for gaining placement for their child.

One of the most popular websites among Singaporean parents these days is called *kiasuparents.com*. It is dedicated to every parent's desire to keep abreast of developments in Singapore's education. Founded by a few parents in 2007, this go-to website for all things relating to education gets around 10,000 unique hits per day.[6] One of the founders created the website precisely because his son could not enroll in a school he thought he could enroll in. The parents did not have the information on how competitive enrolment was for that school at that point in time.[7] This website now provides information on the level of competition to enroll in a particular school, the website's own ranking order of schools, tips for parents in the areas of helping kids prepare for examinations, and even choosing tuition teachers or centres for their children.

Another website, *edumatters.sg*, helps parents gather more information about schools. In this portal, schools are ranked based on reviews by parents themselves.[8] When the MOE did not release the name of the top students for 2012 as its strategy to shift the focus away from academic achievement, parents found other ways to gather the information they wanted.[9] This is how proactive Singaporean parents are in terms of choosing a school for their child! Although MOE has an online School Information Service portal that provides information on school programmes and achievement, many parents still rely on such 'unofficial' portals for extra 'information' to help them in their decision-making process. As one of the founding members of such websites put it, "Being *kiasu* may have negative connotations but parents are *kiasu* because they want to give their children the best".[10] Judging from the large number of parents participating in these websites, one can safely say that *kiasu* parenting is not a phenomenon displayed by a few overly anxious parents in Singapore. It is part of the culture and that culture is all-absorbing. Actions by *kiasu* parents fuel anxiety among others who are not initially *kiasu*. *Kiasu*-ism is a self-reinforcing movement!

Another area that has come to be associated with *kiasu* behaviour is that of parents paying for extra tuition for their children, discussed in Chapter 8. Many would have imagined that these parents pay for extra tuition because their child is academically weak and the child needs extra help to pass examinations. But many students who receive extra tuition are actually doing well in school. The parents just feel more secure in having tuition for their children. It is not about getting an 'A'. It is about making sure that their children get an 'A'. In fact, the headlines of a report in a local newspaper called PSLE "Parents in Singapore Love Extra tuition".[11]

One parent was reported in a local newspaper to have signed her daughter up for tuition six days a week. These after school classes went from 4 p.m. to 9 p.m. The catch was that the daughter regularly scored in the 80s for tests and examinations. But it was not good enough for the mother, who felt that such results would not get her daughter into a top school, or into a school that conducted the International Baccalaureate (IB) programme. Was this a *kiasu* mother, or just one of the many parents in Singapore who were worried about her child's grades?[12]

Hot-housing children as early as preschool is also a manifestation of *kiasu* parenting. One mother, whose son was only five years old and who attended Mandarin lessons four times a week, felt that "in Singapore, you cannot take a laissez-faire attitude".[13] Spending a few thousand dollars per month on tuition for children is not uncommon among Singapore families. Tuition has become an educational arms race, as a local journalist wrote:[14]

> Parents know it doesn't improve their children's grades but they send them for tuition anyway because other children have it. This cycle needs to be broken.

Some parents admitted that they could be the main source of pressure placed upon their children.[15] In an interview study with some 40 parents, one was quoted as saying that "having a childhood is important, but unfortunately, so are grades".[16] Parents send their children, as young as preschool age, to 'enrichment' classes for fear of having their child banded with other children who are lagging behind academically. Many parents believe it is better to over-prepare or at least give them a head start even before they begin primary school.

There is a famous story of how Mencius's mother moved three times for the sake of her son's upbringing. Mencius's mother was one who understood the importance of environment. When Mencius was young, he and his mother lived near a graveyard. Therefore, he played by imitating people digging graves. His mother felt that it was not the right environment for him. They moved to a house near a market. Then Mencius imitated the hawkers selling things. Again his mother felt that it was not the right environment for him. They then shifted to a house near a school. There, Mencius imitated the scholars performing ceremonial rites and formal courtesies. Only then did his mother feel that it was the right environment for him. Of course, Mencius grew up to become a great Confucian scholar. In Singapore, the story is played out by parents moving to get their child into the best primary schools. Because children living near a school get priority enrolment into the school, some parents buy a new property or rent a place that is close to their desired school, just to get priority admission for their child. Indeed, a father pleaded guilty to giving false information to his daughter's prestigious school in order to secure her a place in it.[17]

As a measure to prevent such cases, a ruling was implemented in July 2015. Under the home-school distance category, parents who wish to send their children to their chosen school must abide by the condition that they stay for at least 30 months at the address they have declared at the start of their child's registration.[18] The new regulation received mixed reactions from the public. Some people felt that the 30-month duration was too long and that it might potentially affect the rental prices of homes in the vicinity of popular schools. Others felt that it was a good regulatory move to deter parents from renting homes and moving away immediately after securing a place for their child in school.[19]

Parents under Examination Pressure

Examinations can change families and their lifestyles in Singapore. Sometimes, it seems that the parents are the ones going through the examination, rather than their children. Some parents will put their lives on hold—their careers, work aspirations, and social lives—to focus on helping their children and supporting them through the examination period. A newspaper carried a story of how one mother helped her son deal with examinations. Although she and her husband were both busy with their respective jobs, she chose to cut down a considerable amount of time from work three years before her son was to sit for his PSLE. This meant less overseas work trips, avoiding night-time conference calls, and being home early in the evening, so that she might help her son do consistent revision early on.[20]

Some parents have decided to quit work altogether to give their undivided attention to their child who is sitting for the PSLE. One mother, whose only child struggled with mathematics in primary school, decided to resign from her job to help her daughter prepare for the examinations. Although her daughter already had a private mathematics tutor to help her cope with the subject, she decided to quit work to have more time to coordinate with the tutor and ensure her child had consistent practice at home.[21]

To prepare themselves to help their children, some parents even enroll in enrichment classes and attend workshops to find out more about examination questions and effective strategies in answering those questions. Some parents pay up to S$300 for a three-hour class.[22] These workshops specifically equip parents with skills to teach their children how to score well in the examinations. In a newspaper report, a principal trainer at a learning centre described how this trend grew:[23]

> We started [the tuition centre] in 2009 with lessons only for children. Some time later, we started one workshop for parents a year. Today we conduct six a year, typically in March, June, and November.

Even grandparents can be very much involved in their grandchildren's studies. One grandmother attended an eight-month-long course to help her supervise the studies of her grandchildren. In an interview with a local newspaper, she said:[24]

> My three daughters are grown up and have their own careers. And even though my eldest is a teacher, she is often busy teaching other kids. I thought I should jump in and be involved in my grandchildren's learning processes and growing-up years.

In Singapore, a child's examination is a family affair.

Unreasonable Parents

Parents nowadays are much more educated than they were years ago. Ng Eng Hen, who was then Education Minister, expounded on the rising expectations of well-educated parents:[25]

> Rising educational qualifications will alter the nature of interactions between teacher, student and parent. This change is already occurring as many senior teachers tell me during my school visits. More teachers have requests from parents to customize lessons for their children. Parents are able to discern specific areas of learning difficulties and often are eager to receive regular updates on their child's progress.

The message was echoed more recently by Heng Swee Keat:[26]

Every Parent, a Supportive Partner is not something easy because today we have better educated parents who do not hesitate to make known their expectations and who have sometimes very differing views on what their child's education should be.

Increasing expectations from parents are of course putting a strain on schools. Improving the quality of education is not easy, but it is the rightful duty of a school. However, when education is increasingly seen as a commodity to be consumed, there is a danger. The commoditisation of education fuels the trend of a consumerist education system in which some parents and their children see themselves as customers of schools. When that happens, the deeper and nobler aspects of education begin to erode. It is harder for schools to work in partnership with parents, especially when they have to take an errant child to task.

There have been cases where parents' demands or attitudes were simply unreasonable. Minister Heng told a story about an encounter he had with an irate father who complained about the teachers in his son's school:[27]

> He began his comments with a string of expletives about the teachers in his son's school. With such an attitude in front of me, I could only imagine how he would be like in meeting our teachers. I told him quite firmly that if he wanted us to help him, he must help himself. There is absolutely no reason and no excuse for bad behaviour.

When parents exhibit such behaviour in front of their child, they send a confusing message to their child regarding proper behaviour when dealing with negative emotions. Minister Heng shared another case where a mother filed a police report to complain about her son's teacher for cutting her son's hair:[28]

> More recently, we had a mother who filed a police report and went to the media, aggrieved that her son's $60 haircut was ruined by his teacher. The simple fact is that the son was reminded, over and over again, to trim his hair; and when that failed, the school sent a letter to the parent. The mother's response was that her son was dyslexic and therefore forgetful. Dyslexic people are not forgetful. As one writer put it in a media commentary, by raising such a hullabaloo, "the mother . . . did herself and

her son no favours". If parents do not show graciousness to others and respect for rules, our young will not do so either. Soon, discipline will be eroded, the tone in our schools will deteriorate, and the tone in our society too. Good people will be deterred from joining teaching.

While these examples are isolated cases, they give a picture of what schools have to deal with increasingly.

Engaging Parents as Partners

As part of the strategy in reforming education in Singapore, the MOE actively tries to engage parents to influence their mindsets and get them to embrace holistic education. The MOE has implemented various strategies for parental involvement to achieve this goal—for example, the Parents in Education (PiE) website, Parent Support Group (PSG), and COMmunity and PArents in Support of Schools (COMPASS). By providing parents with various platforms for involvement, the MOE's philosophies are communicated better to them. Parents are also given opportunities to actively participate in the change process.

In 1998, MOE set up the advisory council COMPASS to build and strengthen home-school links.[29] This council comprised representatives from various sectors—schools, business organisations, and self-help groups. Since 1998, more than 95% of schools in the system have set up Parent-Teacher Associations (PTAs) or Parent Support Groups (PSGs).[30] COMPASS, through PTAs and PSGs, works closely with MOE in engaging parents to strengthen home-school partnerships.

The PiE website provides parents with resources and a feedback platform for any issue that concerns their children's education. Parents can also connect with the MOE through parent engagement sessions with MOE officers, via the COMPASS platform. PSGs, which are school-based, are provided with funding for members to organise supportive networks in school among parents, teachers, and students.

In more recent years, the impact of MOE's effort to enhance the effectiveness of PSGs has been manifested in the pervasiveness of parent-led activities, especially in areas such as parent education, coaching of student activities and resource development. It is through these PSGs that parents gain a better understanding of their child, their child's teachers and school policies. Furthermore, they build a network of friends and foster a greater sense of belonging to their child's school and the community at large.[31]

In 2015, the MOE introduced an activity book to support parents of Primary 1 children and help them better manage the transition stage when they have a school-going child. Any parent with a child entering Primary 1 next year will receive a copy in November this year. The book is also available online for teachers. Therefore, parents with children in school are actually very well supported with school-based workshops about parenting, networking sessions with other parents and education experts, and resources both online and in print. In particular, the website Schoolbag.sg also contains useful resources for parents.

Going forward, in line with SkillsFuture, the MOE hopes parents will play a greater role in Education and Career Guidance (ECG). To support parents in this area, the MOE has enhanced the ECG guidebook for parents of students at upper primary and lower secondary levels. The MOE has deployed ECG counsellors at schools, polytechnics, and ITEs to help parents and students make informed choices regarding education and career pathways.

Of course, it is hard to convince parents to change their mindset about academic success until they see clear and undeniable signals that the system is changing. Mindset change does not happen overnight. There is still no better way for parents to feel secure about their children's future than for their children to achieve good examination scores. Even so, despite the many stories of competitive parents, there are signs that mindsets may be changing, albeit slowly. For example, one mother, who went to a prestigious school herself, wrote in the local newspaper that she and her husband had decided to send their daughter to a newly instituted school near their home instead of her alma mater, which was very much sought after. The decision was based on the proximity of the new school to their residence as well as the initial rapport the school had with their daughter when they went to the school's open house event. She said:[32]

> Her school may be a new neighbourhood school but it is staffed by
> dedicated teachers. It may not be a school boasting past stellar results

or a long history, but it is certainly one that best fits my daughter. This is something parents should consider when choosing a school for their children.

Parents' Dilemma in an Education Arms Race

Recently, a teacher spoke with me and told me how she had counselled a couple recently not to feel so stressed up about getting their child into an elite school. The parents were upset that their child's grades were on the borderline of the cut-off points of getting into that school. They were quite determined to get the child into the school and were unhappy that with the results, there was no guarantee of entry. The teacher told me that she tried the tagline of 'Every School, a Good School', but that did not work too well. Then she told me about her own experience. Coincidentally, she was also in the same situation. She had a child of the same age, and her child's grades were on the borderline of the cut-off points in getting into a certain school in which she had always wanted her child to enroll. She told me with a lot of irony that she could do her professional work by advising the parents appropriately. But when it came to her child, she was in a dilemma. She had always wanted her child to enroll in *that* school. Should she persist or should she opt for another school? Then she asked, "Unless things change around here, can you blame the parents?" Singapore parents face a dilemma in an education arms race.

Listen to what one parent has to say in a newspaper commentary:[33]

> It is hard to remain zen and above it all when, all around you, parents are going all out. At which point does one go from being supportive to obsessive, from being a cheerleader to a slave driver? It is frighteningly easy to cross that line because we are all driven by fear. Fear that our kids will lag behind their peers. Fear that this will erode their self-esteem. Fear that this combination of lacklustre results and tattered confidence will doom them to a life of mediocrity . . . We know that the common definition of success is narrow, even inaccurate. But we strive for it nonetheless because while grades, awards and wealth are tangible, measurable and comparable, qualities such as compassion and integrity are not.

The parents' dilemma reminds me of the prisoner's dilemma in game theory. If I am not *kiasu*, and others in the society are not as well, that will be all right. But if I am not *kiasu*, while others in the society are, I will lose out and kick myself for being rather foolish. But how am I supposed to know whether others are *kiasu* or otherwise? If every parent thinks it is 'safer' to be *kiasu*, what will the aggregate effect be?

Conclusion

'Every School, a Good School' is an attempt at setting the society free from the Prisoner's Dilemma of having to deal with escalating competition in the education system. But this needs 'Every Parent, a Supportive Partner', in spirit and in action. There is a silver lining in regard to de-escalating the education arms race in Singapore, as this parent wrote:[34]

> There is hope yet. We can't quit the rat race, but we can set our own rules and pace. The other night, my husband and I sat our son down and spelt out our expectations. We don't expect him to be the best, but we ask that he always tries his best . . . we won't blame him for not understanding what he's taught in school or even failing a subject. But we will suspend his privileges for giving up at the first sign of difficulty or not paying attention in school or at home when we revise the tricky bits with him. . . . In short, even if he doesn't have the aptitude, he should at least get the attitude right.

Many of Singapore's recent education policy initiatives are aimed at addressing culture, rather than just structure. Only time will tell how far the society, in particular the parents, will come to embrace a different education paradigm.

References

1 Heng, S. K. (2014, April 12). Speech by Mr Heng Swee Keat, Minister for Education, at the MOE ExCEL Parent Support Group Conference 2014 at Suntec Convention Centre. Retrieved from http://www.moe.gov.sg/media/speeches/2014/04/12/speech-by-mr-heng-swee-keat-at-the-moe-excel-parent-support-group-conference-2014.php

2 Tan, J. B. & Yates, S. (2011). Academic expectations as sources of stress in Asian students. *Sociology and Psychology in Education*, 14(3), 389–407.

3 Lee, H. L. (2006, August 31). Speech by Prime Minister Lee Hsien Loong at the Teachers' Day Rally 2006, at the Max Pavilion, Singapore Expo. Retrieved from http://www.moe.gov.sg/media/speeches/2006/sp20060831.htm

4 Heng, S. K. (2012, September 12). Keynote Address by Mr Heng Swee Keat, Minister for Education at the Ministry of Education Work Plan Seminar at Ngee Ann Polytechnic Convention Centre. Retrieved from http://www.moe.gov.sg/media/speeches/2012/09/12/keynote-address-by-mr-heng-swee-keat-at-wps-2012.php

5 Tan, P. (2012, June 20). Parent volunteerism scheme discriminates. *Today*, p. 20.

6 Chia, S. (2013, July 1). Kiasu parents prepping P1 registration. *The Straits Times*, p. B4.

7 Heng, L. (2013, July 2). Website a hit with kiasu parents. *The New Paper*, p. 5.

8 Ng, J. Y. (2015, May 22). Portal to rate schools sparks concern among some educators. *Today*, p. 8.

9 Ng, J. Y. & Sreedharan, S. (2012, November 23). PSLE scores still the focus for many parents. *Today*, p. 1.

10 Chia, S. (2013, July 1). Kiasu parents prepping P1 registration. *The Straits Times*, p. B4.

11 Law, Z. T. & Cheow, S. A. (2013, April 29). Parents in Singapore love extra tuition. *The New Paper*, p. 2.

12 Law, Z. T. & Cheow, S. A. (2013, April 29). Parents in Singapore love extra tuition. *The New Paper*, p. 2.

13 Toh, K., Chia, Y. M., & Lua, J. M. (2012, August 28). Without extra lessons, our kids may lose out. *The Straits Times*, p. A7.

14 Davie, S. (2015, July 9). Tuition has become an educational arms race. *The Straits Times*, p. A30.

15 Lee, V. (2015, January 18). Kid's Stress: Whose fault is it? *The Sunday Times Life*, p. 18.

16 Toh, K., Chia, Y. M., & Lua, J. M. (2012, August 28). Without extra lessons, our kids may lose out. *The Straits Times*, p. A7.

17 Poh, I. (2015, January 7). Man lied about address to get daughter into school. *The Straits Times*, p. B6.

18 Ministry of Education (MOE) (2015, May 20). 2015 Primary One Registration Exercise for Admission to Primary One in 2016. Retrieved from http://www.moe.gov.sg/education/admissions/primary-one-registration/

19 Siong, O. (2015, May 26). New primary 1 registration rule for children living near school. *Today Online*. Singapore. Retrieved from http://www.todayonline.com/singapore/new-primary-1-registration-rule-children-living-near-school; Teng, A. (2015, May 26). New P1 admission rule: Live at address for at least 2 ½ years. *The Straits Times*, p. A7.

20 Yong, C. (2012, October 26). Consistent revision is key to less stress. *The Strait Times*, p. B2.

21 Chia, S. (2012, October 26). Mum helps daughter clear Maths hurdle. *The Strait Times*, p. B2.

22 Aw, Y. (2013, August 25). Parents start learning for exams. *The New Paper*, p. 3.
23 Aw, Y. (2013, August 25). Parents start learning for exams. *The New Paper*, p. 3.
24 Aw, Y. (2013, August 25). Parents start learning for exams. *The New Paper*, p. 3.
25 Ng, E. H. (2010, September 6). Opening Address by Dr Ng Eng Hen, Minister for Education and Second Minister for Defence, at the 5th Teachers' Conference 2010 at the Singapore International Convention and Exhibition Centre, Suntec City. Retrieved from http://www.moe.gov.sg/media/speeches/2010/09/06/5th-teachers-conference-2010.php
26 Heng, S. K. (2012, September 12). Keynote Address by Mr Heng Swee Keat, Minister for Education at the Ministry of Education Work Plan Seminar at Ngee Ann Polytechnic Convention Centre. Retrieved from http://www.moe.gov.sg/media/speeches/2012/09/12/keynote-address-by-mr-heng-swee-keat-at-wps-2012.php
27 Heng, S. K. (2012, September 12). Keynote Address by Mr Heng Swee Keat, Minister for Education at the Ministry of Education Work Plan Seminar at Ngee Ann Polytechnic Convention Centre. Retrieved from http://www.moe.gov.sg/media/speeches/2012/09/12/keynote-address-by-mr-heng-swee-keat-at-wps-2012.php
28 Heng, S. K. (2012, September 12). Keynote Address by Mr Heng Swee Keat, Minister for Education at the Ministry of Education Work Plan Seminar at Ngee Ann Polytechnic Convention Centre. Retrieved from http://www.moe.gov.sg/media/speeches/2012/09/12/keynote-address-by-mr-heng-swee-keat-at-wps-2012.php
29 Teo, C. H. (2000, November 17). Speech by RADM (NS) Teo Chee Hean, Minister for Education and Second Minister for Defence at the Ceremony to Commemorate End of COMPASS' First Term of Office and Launch of "Home, School and Community Partnerships" at the Ministry of Education. Retrieved from http://www.moe.gov.sg/media/speeches/2000/sp17112000a.htm
30 Ministry of Education (MOE) (2012). New Website for Parents and Resource Pack for Schools on Home-School-Community Partnership. Press Release. Retrieved from http://www.moe.gov.sg/media/press/2012/09/new-website-for-parents-and-re.php
31 Zulkifli, M. (2009, October 24). Closing Address by Mr Masagos Zulkifli, Senior Parliamentary Secretary, Ministry of Education and Ministry of Home Affairs, at the COMPASS Convention at Temasek Convention Centre, Singapore. Retrieved from http://www.moe.gov.sg/media/speeches/2009/10/24/closing-address-by-mr-masagos.php
32 Louis, I. (2013, August 27). Not "branded" school, but great fit for daughter. *The Straits Times*, p. A23.
33 Tee, H. C. (2015, September 7). Taming the kiasu mother in me. *The Straits Times*, p. B9.
34 Tee, H. C. (2015, September 7). Taming the kiasu mother in me. *The Straits Times*, p. B9.

IV
CONCLUSION

11

LESSONS FROM SINGAPORE

What matters in education reform is a generation of people that is willing to pay the price for change so that the next generation gets a brighter future.

Learning from Singapore's Experiences

What lessons can one distil from Singapore's experiences in educational change? Let us first revisit the four paradoxes and four dreams and draw a lesson from each of them.

Timely Change, Timeless Constants: Education reform should be based on long term consideration of the country's future. It should not be motivated by short-sighted gains or political agenda. Jurisdictions should have the courage to change their education system in a timely manner, while preserving the timeless values that provide beacons to help people navigate the turbulence of change.

Compassionate Meritocracy: A good education system should develop different pathways so that children of different talents can find success in education, regardless of their race, language or religion. Even so, jurisdictions have to look out for those who are left behind. Resources should be allocated so as to level up these children.

Centralised Decentralisation: Jurisdictions should devise a system in which system level synergy can be derived while empowering educators on the ground. The education system should be driven by responsible educators. The accountability system should support responsible educators and not drive their behaviours. In many reforms worldwide, the system sets test-based targets for teachers and school leaders to achieve, but leaves them unsupported and demotivated.

Teach Less, Learn More: Many jurisdictions have made structural changes in their education systems without affecting the teaching and learning processes. Students' experiences have not changed. Education reform should extend its reach into the classroom. It is essential to remind and empower teachers to understand their learners better and develop more suitable pedagogies. More of the same insipid teaching is not the way to inspire better learning!

Every School, a Good School: In a good education system, while schools are different, every school should be able to offer quality education to their students in a safe and conducive school environment. Quality education should not be seen as being offered only by the 'elite' schools. The school system needs to gain the trust of the society over time.

Every Student, an Engaged Learner: Many students are disengaged because lessons are designed by teachers to deliver information to them, without igniting their interest or considering the way they learn. Therefore, teachers should improve their pedagogies and students should be brought into the dynamics of the teaching and learning process in a more meaningful manner.

Every Teacher, a Caring Educator: Building a credible teaching force is not just about attracting the 'best' people to become teachers by offering high salary. It is essential to pay attention to the motivation, professionalism and development of the teaching profession. It is also important to develop a positive image of teachers in the society. A good teaching force is a strategic advantage for the education system and for the entire nation.

Every Parent, a Supportive Partner: The mindset of parents is a very crucial factor in the success of an education system. Therefore, it is essential to work with parents, not just in discussing their child's performance in school but in encouraging a conversation, so that societal culture may shift to support greater commitment to education and children's holistic development.

These lessons are sensible exhortations to any education system. Add them to the ones distilled from international reports (refer to Chapter 1) and one gets a bag full of useful tips for education reform.

But are these the only lessons that the world can learn from Singapore's experiences? Not quite. At first glance, these lessons appear to be strategies that can be easily implemented. But, with a deeper analysis, they are not elementary at all. The way that Singapore has approached these changes matters even more than the changes themselves. In Singapore, educational change is not just about what to do, but how to be. What Singapore does about education reflects the nature of its society and the character of its people. Instead of taking simplistic steps, it faces the tensions in the system and draws strength from the paradoxes for positive change. Instead of policy and practice borrowing, it charts its own path. Instead of following the path of least resistance, it engages with its own culture to challenge entrenched mindsets.

Draw Strength from Paradoxes

Singapore's education system is a microcosm of the society. With children of all races and religion coming together in a common space, the education system affects and is affected by the society profoundly. The education system, probably more than most other systems in the country, is the public arena where abstract values, hidden mindsets and subtle tensions are given their concrete form. The past, present and future, as well as the dynamics at the different levels of the system, are all exerting their influence on the education system. The tensions manifest themselves as paradoxes.

Managing these paradoxes is a critical challenge for Singapore. If managed well, such paradoxes are a source of strength for the system. They generate soul searching discussions and bring the education system forward in a positive evolution. If managed badly, they can become fault lines that polarise Singapore and create disharmony. But this is where Singapore scores. Instead of allowing these paradoxes to be a source of frustration or inhibition, Singapore has been able to draw strength from them. How does Singapore keep a positive direction of change arising from the paradoxes? The answer lies in the unity of purpose.

A united purpose is what holds the Singapore education system together and moves it forward. Singaporeans believe in the importance of education and the need to maintain a good education system, both for the individual and the society. The common education purpose is therefore the beacon by which educators orientate themselves internally while responding to challenges externally. They may have different concerns and they may not agree with certain strategies. But Singapore educators trust in the system and are united in wanting to make things work, rather than to tearing down the edifice. That is why paradoxes are creative tensions, rather than destructive ones, and result in positive movements rather than negativity or disintegration.

The driving power of a common purpose is enhanced by the close-knit nature of the education fraternity. The officials from MOE, teachers from schools, and teacher educators from NIE are constantly interacting through official and invisible networks about educational policies, school practices and teacher development. Such discussions are not always harmonious. Sometimes, they can be filled with ambiguities, contradictions and a plurality of beliefs. But the important thing is that Singapore is able to take this in its stride. Through close interactions and intimate dialogues, the dissonance caused by these paradoxes is converted into positive energy that is channeled into shaping the system in a negotiated direction. Change emerges through a process of advocacy, nudging and mutual understanding, by parties united by a common purpose of education and nation building. With these parameters, the system evolves in a positive direction.

This intensity of interaction and the close interconnectedness also give the system its cultural ballast to weather change. When challenges come as a perturbation to the system, the education community pulls on one another for mutual support, much like the threads of a net. The system absorbs the perturbation. In doing so, it transforms and emerges more resilient. It is theoretically possible that a perturbation in a system is greater than its adaptive capacity and will cause it to break apart. That explains why Singapore is always careful and calculating in approaching change, so that change will strengthen the system, not dismantle it.

Being pragmatic has both advantages and disadvantages. But in the area of educational change, the pragmatic nature of Singaporeans actually enhances the driving power of a common purpose. With any change, a common purpose does not mean that everyone thinks the same way about the means to the end. The root of some of these differences can be deeply visceral, and some issues do not have an easy common ground. But disharmony has not been the way to end differences in the Singapore education community. The pragmatic Singaporean educator complains about certain dissonances, accepts the paradoxes, and moves on. Most educators do not find value in repeatedly discussing rhetoric that leads nowhere. Singapore's history has shaped Singaporeans. Philosophy is important but people are not obsessed with it. The more important questions are, does it work? What are the pros and cons? Do the benefits outweigh the risks? That is the Singaporean way.

There is a concern that the very nature of pragmatism may stifle discussion, participation and human agency. However, in Singapore, this seems to play out in a different way in the education system. There is discussion, participation and human agency. But there is a general acceptance that there needs to be hard-nosed decision-making and unity to make things work. To many Singapore educators, it is pointless to discuss an issue endlessly and be paralysed by these discussions. Singapore is more interested in movements amid reflective contestations, rather than in paralysis amid protracted discussions.

Actually, pragmatism is not a Singaporean invention. Pragmatism, as a philosophy which focuses on utility and practicality instead of dogmatic intellectualism, began in the United States in the 1870s, promoted by Charles Sanders Peirce and William James. But Singapore has honed pragmatism rather artistically into a culture. The education system is changing because pragmatic Singapore knows that it is untenable not to change! But the change must be practical. Ideas that cannot be implemented are not helpful! The end result is paradoxically both rapid change and relative stability in the system. Singapore's quest of challenging the norms and having dogged adherence to practicality explains the momentum of change in the quality aspects of the system and the relative stability in the structure of the system to support those changes.

Finds Its Own Path

Policy and practice borrowing is quite prevalent globally, but Singapore believes in finding its own path. There are many other successful systems in the world. Finland's way of equity has helped the country do very well in its education.[1] Equity in Finland is admirable, but Singapore does not try to become Finland (and indeed Finland should not try to become Singapore).[2] If Singapore were to copy Finland, some citizens may become concerned with whether the brightest students will be held back because of equity in the education system. In compassionate meritocracy, Singapore has developed its own interpretation of equity, so that no child is left behind or held back.

While others in the world are emphasising standardised tests and examination results, Singapore is going the other way. Singapore does not copy what may appear to be the current global flavor, but considers the needs of the next generation of its people. 'Timely Change, Timeless Constants' attests to this spirit. Singapore has changed its education system in a sure and steady way, over many years. But these moves are motivated to build a nation. They are not motivated by face-saving politics to hold on to an ineffective policy or show people that there is a change by wiping the slate clean for every change of office-bearer.

Singapore does believe in learning from others, but it is sensitive to its own context when doing so. Each year, Singapore sponsors many teachers and school leaders on overseas learning trips. But the aim of such trips is not to import policies or practices. Rather, the idea is to understand the principles behind the success of others and to use the observations of a different system to trigger these educators to reflect deeply about the way that they think. Some elite schools from the West are superb in bringing out the creativity in a select group of children. Singapore schools, on the other hand, must cater to all children in an accessible and affordable way as a national system. So, in learning from these schools overseas, the average Singapore school tries to understand the principles behind the practices and adapts ideas suitably to cater to a wide spectrum of learner abilities, aptitude, personalities and home backgrounds.

According to Yong Zhao, Chinese leaders are frustrated with their schools, which can produce excellent test-takers but not innovative entrepreneurs. American policy makers are also frustrated with their schools, some of which cannot produce students who can ace standardised tests, despite an economy that thrives on different kinds of creativity rather than qualifications.[3] Singapore does not want to go either way. Singapore is moving away from very narrowly-defined educational outcomes, based only on examinations in key subject areas, towards a more holistic education system that can encourage creativity. But it is cautious not to throw out the baby with the bath water. It understands its own context and intends to find its own path to enter new spaces in a sure-footed manner without sacrificing its core strengths.

Unlike the knee-jerk reactions that one observes in some other parts of the world, Singapore believes in reforming its education system systemically and systematically. In other words, reform is coherent throughout the system and is carried out with clear methodology. Policy, practice and preparation are all addressed. Actually, this is a reflection of the way of governance in Singapore. As an example, in 2015, a senior minister was appointed to oversee and coordinate cross-ministry efforts in each of the three major areas of change in the country—namely, national security, economic and social policies, and infrastructure. This facilitates the implementation of a systemic and systematic approach in responding to increasingly complex issues that involve multiple ministries. Moreover, these senior ministers then become 'mentors' to new ministers who have come into specific ministries. This allows change and continuity, all at the same time.

Singapore follows through on its plans with order and method. The MOE has systematically followed through the implementation of 'Every School, a Good School' in 2012, 'Every Student, an Engaged Learner' in 2013, 'Every Teacher, a Caring Educator' in 2014 and 'Every Parent, a Supportive Partner' in 2015. The focus of the interventions shifts systematically through the years 2012 to 2015. Long-suffering is a virtue in educational change. Singapore demonstrates patience in seeing through a long term plan step by step.

Engage with Its Own Culture

Singapore understands that the nature of education is influenced by societal culture. If educational change to embrace holistic education and broaden the definition of success is to succeed, the existing competitive culture and grade-focused mindset have to change. Many jurisdictions make changes to systems and structures without addressing the cultural factors. But Singapore demonstrates the courage to engage with its own culture. Going against entrenched mindsets is seldom a popular move.

One of the beliefs that Singapore is trying to change in the society is that qualifications are all that matter to land a good career and prosper in life. However, this belief is not always valid. Initial qualifications may help one to open the first door, but it will not guarantee lifetime employment or progression. Many jobs require a person to keep on acquiring new knowledge or deeper skills on the job. Whether one is a chef or a software programmer, one will need to upgrade knowledge and skills continuously, or be made irrelevant to the industries. Therefore, qualifications do matter but they are not life insurances. What is more necessary is to develop in young people the attitude of lifelong learning and adaptability to keep learning and improving.

The current tuition boom is precisely the phenomenon suggesting that efforts at changing societal culture need to be doubled. The problem is that, nowadays, tuition is no longer an extra help for a child to pass examinations. Instead, a lot of children who are actually doing well in school are receiving extra tuition. This is a perpetual attempt by parents to get their children to perform at increasingly higher levels to get in front of other children. This is a never-ending race. The only way to stop it is to challenge Singaporeans' fundamental beliefs about how a good life can be achieved.

The four dreams are not just visions but also attempts to address the aspects of Singapore's culture that inhibit educational change. 'Every School, a Good School' speaks against the culture of excessive competition to gain entry into 'elite' schools. 'Every Student, an Engaged Learner' shifts the focus of education from grades to learning. 'Every Teacher, a Caring Educator' emphasises the important role of teachers in an age where respect for teachers is in danger of eroding. 'Every Parent, a Supportive Partner' signifies how the school system needs the support of parents and the community for education to succeed.

The Singapore experience illustrates to the world that education reform is deeply entwined with societal culture. It is never 'merely' an education issue. But Singapore demonstrates the courage to take the more difficult path, confront its own cultural issues, face the tensions and find its own solutions.

The Journey Ahead for Singapore's Education System

Throughout Singapore's history, the education system has played a critical role in national development. The challenges facing the education system are tied closely to the social and economic situation of Singapore. This has not changed and is unlikely to change in the future. The journey ahead for Singapore's education system will therefore be as tough as that during the days of nation building. New challenges will arise because of changing realities in the economic and social realms. A few examples will serve to illustrate the tensions that the education system will have to deal with.

First, there will be an increasing tension regarding the nature of education. On one hand, Singapore is promoting holistic education. On the other hand, Singapore needs to achieve depth in the various scientific disciplines in order to compete in the high-end industries, such as those in life sciences, biomedical and pharmaceutical sectors. On one hand, Singapore is trying to reduce the competitiveness within the education system. On the other hand, Singapore needs to increase its competitiveness as an economy because it is competing with bigger and more mature economies, and it does not have their economic ballast. While these are not necessarily irreconcilable conflicts, there will be demands from different directions upon a curriculum that is already tightly packed. Everything seems to be important but wise choices have to be made.

Second, Singapore has been successful and success leads to expectations. Many people want to upgrade their qualifications. But Singapore must avoid a situation where a so-called first-class education system graduates many people with advanced qualifications but without jobs in the market for them. In South Korea, for example, there are now too many graduates chasing too few jobs. Because of their high qualifications, these young people are reluctant to accept a job that seems to be traditionally beneath a university graduate. Therefore, qualifications can set up expectations that the economy may not able to fulfil. This creates social problems. Prime Minister Lee Hsien Loong said:[4]

> We should not just churn out graduates regardless of the quality or the employment opportunities—set up the institutions, run the courses, print the degrees, produce the graduates, generate a lot of disappointment

and unhappiness. Other countries have made this mistake—you produce unemployed graduates, underemployed graduates. Europe has got
them, Britain, America, even China, many graduates come out looking
for work, cannot find work.

Therefore, Singapore needs to find the delicate balance so that a
discourse that encourages aspiration will not result in subsequent dis-
satisfaction and a discourse for managing expectations will not result
in demotivation. The challenge is to encourage aspiration and manage
expectations at the same time.

Third, Singapore needs more innovations and entrepreneurial
activities, but such undertakings involve taking risks. There is no certainty of success, but there is a certainty of hard work to walk a path
less travelled. Here, the pragmatic nature of Singaporeans becomes
an inhibitor. Singaporeans are educated to be pragmatic and rational
thinkers. When they are young, they are advised by their teachers to
answer the easy questions first in an examination. Secure the points.
Do not waste time on questions they are not sure about. So when
they become adults, they think through their career choices in the
same way. Should they try something if the associated risks are great?
Even when they are willing to take some risks, they would like a safety
net—a government scheme to support their effort. So, support from
the top, while critical from a certain perspective, can result in reliance
in the long run. The tricky question is to figure out how young people
may be encouraged to be innovative and entrepreneurial against the
existing cultural grain, through the right platforms of support, without
them being reliant on such support in the long run.

Fourth, the government has been interventionist in its policy when
it comes to developing a system that brings education to all. The worry
is that left to 'ground-up' forces, change may not be quick enough or
may be uneven in the system. However, moving forward, the education system has to be more flexible and agile, sustained by continuous
extensive knowledge creation, usage and renewal capabilities, not just
from the top but throughout the system. Policy makers have to manage the education system as a complex adaptive system rather than a
machine. Such a system has a 'life' of its own. People organise themselves to do good work. The transformation of the education system is

more organic, and there is a higher level of initiation from the ground up. At this moment, important areas of change are identified by the government. But to develop a more mature education system, it is important that an organic self-organising paradigm[5] can subsequently emerge so that schools have greater resilience in facing the challenges of a pluralistic society and have a greater capacity for change. Singapore is already making the paradigmatic shift and venturing into a new mode of thinking which embraces higher levels of complexity, so that its education system may be adaptable and forward-looking. But getting the balance right is the tricky question. If the degree of freedom is too low, the self-organising dynamics will be inhibited and creativity limited. If the degree of freedom is too high, the system may move into a dysfunctional state where synergy as a system is lost.

Fifth, values provide an anchor as economic conditions fluctuate and world powers rise and fade. But it will be increasingly challenging to implement values education in Singapore as the society becomes more and more pluralistic. Whose values shall it adopt? Even if Singapore can 'standardise' the values, can such values be transmitted effectively? Values education requires role-modelling, but it is increasingly clear that different generations of teachers have different values or different standards of similar values. Similarly, it will be increasingly challenging to implement citizenship education in Singapore. A challenge that comes because of Singapore's success is that the younger generation of Singaporeans, who have only known a prosperous Singapore, do not realise how unnatural that prosperity is and how difficult the effort was to create that prosperity. Some are skeptical of citizenship education, perceiving it as propaganda to keep citizens obedient to authority. But in the long run, the responsibility to ensure that Singapore can continue to thrive for many years to come must rest on the shoulders of those who are young now, and whether they have a good grasp of what is and is not viable for a small country. Both values and citizenship education cannot be ritualised, but they are part of a strategy to transmit the national DNA. The challenge is to figure out how critical messages can be transmitted subtly but clearly.

In all these areas, Singapore is likely to exhibit behaviours that will appear paradoxical because it will be negotiating competing demands, each of which comes with valid reasoning, and when taken together offer no easy common grounds. Paradoxically, because these are great challenges, there is great hope for Singapore. Because policy makers, school leaders and teachers can accept and navigate paradoxes, their aggregated movement will ensure that the system will never 'settle' into a state of homeostasis. Instead, Singapore will thrive by capitalising on its skills of walking the tightrope, a competency that it has honed over the years of nation building.

Can Singapore Be a Model?

Can another country or jurisdiction learn from Singapore? Possibly, even though the scale can be quite different. However, there is a Chinese saying that although the sparrow is small, it must have all its organs. Whether an eagle or a sparrow, a system must have its full complement of parts and these parts must work well together! This is what Singapore is strong at—education reform takes place at the system, school, classroom and individual levels. Every part of the system is integrated and interacts intensely together to develop and implement a coherent and sustainable action plan. It is relatively easy to find an excellent school somewhere in a system. It is much harder to find an excellent school system. This is what Singapore is constantly changing to become—an excellent system of schools for all, not a system with some excellent schools for a few.

I would not call Singapore a *model* education system per se. Singapore's education system is not perfect. The citizen of another country with a more liberal education system will hardly be excited at the extent to which parents in Singapore will go to help their children succeed in school. Compared with many others, Singapore's education system is still rather top-down, examination-oriented, competitive and stressful for students. In early childhood and special education, it is still trying to catch up with systems in other countries that are more advanced in these areas. However, its commitment to educational excellence for all, long term planning, careful implementation, system coherence, teacher professional development and confronting inhibiting mindsets should inspire other systems to reflect on their own. Learning from Singapore is not about transferring policies and practices. Similar to what Singapore has done to learn from others, an observation of educational change in Singapore can help other systems question their own beliefs and change certain mindsets. Let me offer some 'what if' reflective questions for different education systems, based on Singapore's experience (of course, please consider only the questions that are appropriate):

1 What if education can be seen by the whole country as an investment rather than an expenditure?
2 What if education reform can be planned with a long term perspective and followed through faithfully, even when there is a change in the political office-holder?
3 What if there is a way for different parties to work together to achieve greater coherence and synergy in policy, practice and preparation in the education system?
4 What if the country is committed to making quality education available to *all*, rather than just to *some*?
5 What if teachers are seen as nation builders rather than professionals of low status?
6 What if there is a commitment in the education system to recruit and develop good teachers and school leaders?
7 What if education reform is committed towards helping teachers improve teaching and helping students become more engaged in learning, rather than just making structural changes?
8 What if teachers and schools are evaluated by their professional efforts at educating and caring for their students holistically, and not by their students' test scores?
9 What if society is willing to confront its culture to facilitate a national commitment to excellence in education?
10 What if education becomes a much more positive and uplifting narrative in the country, rather than being berated often in the media and other social spaces?

In an educational change, every intervention has its benefits and consequences. No education reform is going to satisfy everyone. Therefore, any education reform is a contested process. It tests the will of a people. There will be paradoxes, embedded with tensions. The results will show whether the reform is merely about shouting a slogan or seriously about fighting a mission. If it is the former, it will soon die a natural death. If it is the latter, people will rally together and bite the bullet for the next generation. The Singapore experience raises the most fundamental question about any education reform: Is it *real*?

Conclusion

Founding Prime Minister Lee Kuan Yew passed away early in the morning on 23 March 2015. Given his stature in the country, many would have predicted an impact on investors' confidence and Singapore's economy. Significantly, the country's stock market held steady. Mr Lee's legacy is precisely this: what could have been a shock wave for the economy went through as ripples. The muted impact is a testament to the strength of the country. Even the market recognises Singapore's psychological depth, the smooth handover of power in a non-corrupt government and the tenacity of its people.

The passing of Lee Kuan Yew was both a heart-breaking and yet uplifting episode in Singapore's history. People queued up in an orderly fashion for more than 8 hours just to pay their respects to the man instrumental in the founding of Singapore. They organised themselves and gave one another support to last the queue. Shopkeepers in the vicinity offered free drinks, snacks and umbrellas on their own accord. Hundreds of thousands of people came onto the streets to mourn and honour the founding prime minister. Lee's passing had a profound effect on Singaporeans. It was a time of mourning. It was a time of soul searching. Never in recent history had the history of how Singapore survived been so pertinent to the young and old. It was not expected. When Lee Kuan Yew was alive, many people went about their lives without showing much appreciation. When he was gone, the outpouring of gratitude was tremendous. Beneath the pragmatic Singaporean spirit, there is a sentimental Singaporean soul.

Singapore, as a nation, is just half a century old, having celebrated its 50th birthday in 2015. But it has undergone tremendous changes despite its tender age. Singapore's story is about a group of people who strive to be versatile enough to adapt to the rapid changes in the world. Singapore could have been led by a noose, but it chose to control its destiny. After five decades of nation building, it has a thriving economy with a high per capita income and tops the OECD's global education ranking. Sustaining Singapore's success over the next 50 years will be trickier and more demanding than the transformation of Singapore over the past 50 years. For Singapore to continue leading the way in the quality of education, it needs to muster the same combination of shrewd resourcefulness, courage and tenacity shown by its pioneering generation, who has overcome the odds of survival and thrived on the challenges of their time. Singapore cannot stand still. It cannot afford to. It needs to continue to adapt and develop new strengths. Being a small country means that there is little room for complacency and margin for error. Yet, being overly careful will just inhibit the creativity and maturity process of the society. Tough judgement calls and hard choices lie ahead of Singapore.

At this time, guide books providing model answers to past-year examination questions are still best-sellers in bookstores. There are some in the world who may say that Singapore students are obsessed with grades and are shaped to be risk-averse. Others may say that Singapore students are the world's best problem solvers. Regardless of what the world thinks, Singapore knows the strengths and weaknesses of its education system. It has the gumption to make changes for improvement. What matters in such a change is a generation of people that is willing to weather the difficulties of change so that the next generation gets a brighter future.

I have travelled to many parts of the world giving speeches at international conferences. I have told many audiences that in 50 years' time, if there was a similar conference, their country would be represented at the conference. Would Singapore be there in 50 years' time? As a citizen, I certainly hope so! Singapore has beaten the odds to survive and prosper, and will beat the odds again for another 50 years or more. I may not be alive in 50 years to see Singapore well and prosperous. But I am quietly confident it will be. By that time, I hope there will be another book by someone else to celebrate the struggles and achievements of Singapore and its education system. Please wish us well!

References

1 Sahlberg, P. (2011). *Finnish Lessons: What Can the World Learn from Educational Change in Finland?* New York: Teachers College Press.

2 Ng, P. T. & Hargreaves, A. (2013, July 9). Singapore should not be Finland. *Today*, pp. 14–16.
3 Zhao, Y. (2012). *World Class Learners: Educating Creative and Entrepreneurial Students.* Thousand Oaks: Corwin Press.
4 Lee, H. L. (2012). A Home with Hope and Heart. Prime Minister Lee Hsien Loong's National Day Rally 2012. Retrieved from http://www.pmo.gov.sg/mediacentre/prime-minister-lee-hsien-loongs-national-day-rally-2012-speech-english
5 Ng, P. T. (2009). Examining the use of new science metaphors in learning organisation. *The Learning Organization*, 16(2), 168–180.

Index

Note: figures and tables are denoted with italicized page numbers.

193

Taylor & Francis eBooks

Helping you to choose the right eBooks for your Library

Add Routledge titles to your library's digital collection today. Taylor and Francis ebooks contains over 50,000 titles in the Humanities, Social Sciences, Behavioural Sciences, Built Environment and Law.

Choose from a range of subject packages or create your own!

Benefits for you

» Free MARC records
» COUNTER-compliant usage statistics
» Flexible purchase and pricing options
» All titles DRM-free.

REQUEST YOUR FREE INSTITUTIONAL TRIAL TODAY

Free Trials Available
We offer free trials to qualifying academic, corporate and government customers.

Benefits for your user

» Off-site, anytime access via Athens or referring URL
» Print or copy pages or chapters
» Full content search
» Bookmark, highlight and annotate text
» Access to thousands of pages of quality research at the click of a button.

eCollections – Choose from over 30 subject eCollections, including:

Archaeology	Language Learning
Architecture	Law
Asian Studies	Literature
Business & Management	Media & Communication
Classical Studies	Middle East Studies
Construction	Music
Creative & Media Arts	Philosophy
Criminology & Criminal Justice	Planning
Economics	Politics
Education	Psychology & Mental Health
Energy	Religion
Engineering	Security
English Language & Linguistics	Social Work
Environment & Sustainability	Sociology
Geography	Sport
Health Studies	Theatre & Performance
History	Tourism, Hospitality & Events

For more information, pricing enquiries or to order a free trial, please contact your local sales team:
www.tandfebooks.com/page/sales

 Routledge
Taylor & Francis Group

The home of
Routledge books

www.tandfebooks.com

Made in the USA
Middletown, DE
28 February 2024

50523176R00117